Social and Political Representations of the COVID-19 Crisis

Weaving together political, sociological, psychological, and epidemiological analyses, *Social and Political Representations of the COVID-19 Crisis* provides revealing insights into the transformations wrought by the pandemic and the social divisions it has exposed. Accounting for the realities of the pandemic across the globe, with a strong focus on experiences in the Global South, this book challenges readers to question their beliefs about the societies they live in and how these societies should respond to collective catastrophes. Originally published in Spanish, this English edition is thoroughly revised and updated.

Social and Political Representations of the COVID-19 Crisis analyzes the varied strategies attempted in different parts of the world to deal with the pandemic, including elimination, mitigation, flattening the curve, and herd immunity, and the ramifications of these approaches. It argues that the different strategies are guided by social representations that can be analyzed on epistemological, emotional, and ethical-moral levels. Drawing upon a wide range of thinkers, the book also investigates the key role of psychological defense mechanisms, including different ways of denying the seriousness of the pandemic and different paranoid responses to pain and frustration, such as scapegoating and conspiracy theories.

This timely book analyzes the transformations in the social fabric brought about by the pandemic and the questions it poses for the future of our societies. It will therefore be of great interest to students and researchers in the humanities, social sciences, and public health, as well as the general reader.

Daniel Feierstein is Director of the Centre of Genocide Studies at the National University of Tres de Febrero, Argentina, and Director of the Observatory of State Crimes at the University of Buenos Aires, Argentina. He is also Senior Researcher at the National Research Council of Argentina (CONICET). His work primarily focuses on genocidal social practices and has been crucial in the increased recognition of the Argentine military junta's crimes as genocide. He is a previous president of the International Association of Genocide Scholars and has acted as a judge on the Permanent People's Tribunal in Sri Lanka, Mexico, Myanmar, and Colombia. He is the author of several books, including *Genocide as a Social Practice: Reorganizing Society under the Nazis and Argentina's Military Juntas* (Rutgers University Press, 2014) and *Memorias y Representaciones: Sobre la elaboracion del genocidio I* (FCE, 2012). During the COVID-19 pandemic, Feierstein participated in numerous national and provincial advisory councils in Argentina assessing the social aspects of the crisis.

Douglas Andrew Town is a British-born translator and writer. He lives in Buenos Aires, Argentina, where he directs the Master in Translation program at the University of Belgrano. He has translated numerous books and articles from Spanish, German, and French in various areas of the humanities and social sciences. He published his first novel, *Southern Waters*, in 2019.

The COVID-19 Pandemic Series

Series Editor: *J. Michael Ryan*

This series examines the impact of the COVID-19 pandemic on individuals, communities, countries, and the larger global society from a social scientific perspective. It represents a timely and critical advance in knowledge related to what many believe to be the greatest threat to global ways of being in more than a century. It is imperative that academics take their rightful place alongside medical professionals as the world attempts to figure out how to deal with the current global pandemic, and how society might move forward in the future. This series represents a response to that imperative.

Titles in this Series:

Social and Political Representations of the COVID-19 Crisis

Daniel Feierstein

Translated by Douglas Andrew Town

LONDON AND NEW YORK

First published 2023
by Routledge
4 Park Square, Milton Park, Abingdon, Oxon OX14 4RN

and by Routledge
605 Third Avenue, New York, NY 10158

Routledge is an imprint of the Taylor & Francis Group, an informa business

© 2023 Daniel Feierstein

British Library Cataloguing-in-Publication Data
A catalogue record for this book is available from the British Library

Library of Congress Cataloging-in-Publication Data
A catalog record has been requested for this book

ISBN: 978-1-032-21280-7 (hbk)
ISBN: 978-1-032-21279-1 (pbk)
ISBN: 978-1-003-26761-4 (ebk)

DOI: 10.4324/9781003267614

Typeset in Times New Roman
by Deanta Global Publishing Services, Chennai, India

Contents

Foreword

When news of the first cases of the new SARS-CoV-2 virus began to emerge in late 2019 and early 2020, there were few people who would have predicted the radical changes the world was about to experience, much less the rapid speed at which those changes would be brought about. Classrooms became ghost towns while living rooms became offices. Bandwidth became an issue of serious social concern and Zoom fatigue gained medical recognition. And that was just for the lucky ones. For those not so lucky, education stopped, as did paychecks. Social encounters became fraught with concern, and not without merit, as they were now risky encounters with a potentially disabling, deadly virus.

It is important to distinguish between the SARS-CoV-2 virus, an infectious agent best understood by medical professionals, and the COVID-19 pandemic, the social, cultural, economic, and psychological impact of the spread, and efforts to contain, the virus, an issue perhaps best understood by social scientists. Since the beginning of the pandemic, medical professionals have been forced to act as politicians while politicians have been masquerading as medical professionals. The fact that basic scientifically proven means of mitigating, even eliminating, the virus – masks, physical distancing, vaccines – have become political issues speaks to the destructive power, and deadly consequences, of the politicization of medicine. The virus doesn't check voter registration records before infection, and calculated responses to a pandemic should not involve considerations of political gain. In short, lives should be more important than votes, though in many places that has sadly not been the case.

As a response to the call for social scientists to lend our expertise to pandemic concerns, I started The COVID-19 Pandemic Series, of which the book you are reading is a welcome addition. In fact, it is exactly the kind of scholarship I had hoped for when starting the series. Feierstein has lent his decades of expertise as a leading scholar of genocide studies to provide insights into responses to the pandemic from a social, psychological, political, and in all ways, social justice perspective. As Feierstein so aptly notes, the pandemic can either be an opportunity for us to imagine a different, more just, more environmentally sustainable form of society, or it can be an experience that only serves to reinforce hegemonic capitalist interests and exacerbates existing inequalities. The choice, in short, is up to us. If we listen carefully to the insightful analysis of Feierstein, then it might not (yet) be too late to make the right one.

J. Michael Ryan
Series Editor, The COVID-19 Pandemic Series
February 2022

Acknowledgments

Academic publishing is very much a collective endeavor, and the acknowledgments section is where authors try (albeit inadequately) to recognize at least some of their debts. Like many others, this book was only possible thanks to a very large number of researchers, colleagues, and friends, and a complete list of acknowledgments would be endless. I therefore apologize in advance if I have forgotten anybody in the maelstrom of this second year defined by the COVID-19 outbreak.

This book owes its genesis to Malena Silveyra, Iván Fina, and Adriana Taboada, who played an essential role both in developing many of the ideas in it and editing the drafts of the Spanish edition. Adriana and Iván provided invaluable psychoanalytic insights, and Malena's long comments on each chapter helped me avoid dozens of epistemological and political inaccuracies, making for a more solid text. Any errors remaining in this area or any other are entirely my own.

In spite of all the suffering the pandemic has brought, these past two years have also been enormously enriching thanks to contacts with professionals from other disciplines, including the exact sciences and medicine as well as the human sciences. In this regard I would like to mention my endless conversations with Roberto Etchenique and Guillermo "Willy" Durán, the common work for a proposal of "selective, planned and intermittent isolations," and the voluntary work team created for this purpose with Rodrigo Castro, Ernesto Kofman, and Omar Sued. Also of great importance was Jorge Aliaga's most welcome invitation to join various discussion groups, where I learned every day from important researchers in the most diverse fields, including Jorge himself (a scientist of boundless curiosity and willing to become involved in social issues) but also Zacarías Bustos, Florencia and Leandro Cahn, Humberto Debat, Juan Flo, Juan Fraire, Diego Garbervetsky, Daniela Hozbor, Alberto Kornblihtt, Mario Lozano, Rodrigo Maidana, Franco Mársico, Sol Minoldo, Nicolás and Santiago Olszevicki, Rodrigo Quiroga, Ernesto Resnik, Soledad Retamar, Carlos Stortz, Gustavo

Tiffenberg, and Sebastián Uchitel. It is also worth mentioning the immense contribution of a talented group of science journalists, a profession that has not been valued enough in the context of this crisis. Members of this group who found time to talk to me include Nora Bär, Natalia Concino, Diana Constanzo, Ana Correa, Florencia Cunzolo, Pablo Esteban, Andrea Gentil, Emilse Pizarro, Valeria Román, and Sonia Santoro. But I am probably forgetting many others who contributed to rich and interesting debates of all kinds.

The seminars at the Institute of Calculus and the Institute of Scientific Computing at the University of Buenos Aires (UBA) chaired by Willy Durán and Diego Garbervetsky proved to be fruitful learning environments. The October 1, 2020 meeting was a golden opportunity to discuss at a very early stage some of the concepts presented in this book.

In the social sciences, exchanges with Ricardo Aronskind, Verónica Giménez-Beliveau, Verónica Giordano, Alejandro Grimson, Gabriel Kessler, Hugo Lewin, Mario Pecheny, Cecilia Rossi, and Ariel Wilkis were most enlightening, and many discussions are still ongoing. While I was finishing this book, Javier Balsa's invitation to take part in research carried out by the PISAC-COVID-19 project was also of enormous value, as were the results that began to emerge in late 2020. The project is based at the Institute on Contemporary Argentine Economy and Society (IESAC) of the National University of Quilmes, where Javier directs multiple social science research nodes. These results are included in the book although in less depth than they deserve. The same goes for Javier's detailed and insightful critique of a previous draft of this book, which I was able to take advantage of during the final proofreading for the Spanish edition.

Over the last five years, I have been invited to many interesting debates within the disciplines of psychiatry, psychology, and psychoanalysis. The second half of 2020 included numerous information sharing days devoted to many of the topics developed in this book. I would especially like to highlight my conversations with Silvia Bentolila, Yago Franco, and Nicolás Vallejo, and the interesting day we spent together with Ernesto Calvo, a day organized by the College of Psychoanalysts, discussing the role of social networks in the context of pandemics, as well as invitations from the Argentine Association of Psychology and Group Psychotherapy, the Argentine Psychoanalytical Association (APA), the Psychoanalytic Association of Buenos Aires (Apdeba), and the Argentine Work and Research Team (EATIP), among many others. I owe an enormous debt to each and every one of the human rights organizations in Argentina but most especially to the survivors of the Argentine genocide for what they have taught me over a space of three decades, and to José Schulman, of the Argentine League for Human Rights, for our talks during the pandemic.

I would like to thank Mario Kligman, who departed this life in 2020, for repeatedly reminding me of the value of indignation in the face of injustice. I miss him tremendously.

Since the beginning of the pandemic, I have been in frequent touch with my cousin Haydée Bujman-Lancman, a physician who has lived in the United States for several decades. These conversations gave rise to some of the first questions in this book. Throughout 2020, I also received reports from my sister, Liliana Feierstein, on the social, political, and health situation in Germany, which provided a particularly useful contrast with Latin America.

An important inspiration for this book came from working with the Health Research Area of the Gino Germani Institute and the Hogares de Cristo. I began working with them in 2018 and we came up with many creative initiatives to deal with the pandemic – for example, the proposal for community quarantines in February 2020, which was accepted by the Argentine authorities. Much of what is analyzed in this book stems from those early debates and from a wonderful group made up of Ana Laura Azparren, Ana Clara Camarotti, Eva Camelli, Fabiola Carcar, Alejandro Capriati, Martín Güelman, Hugo Fernández, Adriana Taboada, and Pablo Vidal. Together with experts from the Center for Genocide Studies of the National University of Tres de Febrero (UNTREF), we formed the so-called "Health, social relations and subjective structures in situations of vulnerability" team in March 2020. We made recommendations to political decision-making bodies in the first months and then participated in the drawing up of a proposal for Selective, Planned, and Intermittent Isolations (ASPI) which we submitted to the Argentine government in July 2020. In mid-2020, I was invited onto various advisory committees (one in which I still participate advises the government of the province of Buenos Aires) and to numerous evaluation meetings with different areas of national, provincial, and municipal government. There, I was able to gather a lot of information, contribute ideas from the social sciences for the implementation of health policies, and learn about the difficulties and problems of state management. I would like to highlight my conversations with Facundo Ramos (Director of Planning in the Ministry of Governmental Affairs of Formosa, Argentina), regarding the way in which the province of Formosa faced the fight against the pandemic and the difficulties experienced by the provincial government in the first months of 2021. The meeting arranged by Rodolfo Kaufmann with members of the contact tracing and isolation teams of the telemedicine centers (CETEC) opened at the UNTREF was also particularly illuminating.

I would particularly like to mention the generosity of *El Cohete a la Luna* in communicating some of my early contributions to these debates during 2020 and the interest of numerous journalists in many of the issues raised in my interventions in articles and social networks.

As always, I am grateful for the permanent institutional support of the National Council for Scientific and Technical Research (CONICET) and the authorities of the UNTREF (Aníbal Jozami, Martín Kaufmann, Carlos Mundt, Pablo Jacovkis, Hamurabi Noufouri, and Raúl Sánchez Antelo) in an institution where I have always felt at home. The same goes for the enthusiastic and committed participation of all the members of the CEG at the UNTREF and the Observatory of State Crimes at the Faculty of Social Sciences of the UBA. I am grateful, too, to the director of the Sociology Department of the UBA, Hugo Lewin, for his support and advice and to the technical coordinators of the CEG, Facundo Giménez and Claudia Massuh, for their untiring encouragement and the quality of their work.

Thanks go, also, to Gastón Levin and Mariana Rey, from Fondo de Cultura Económica, for convincing me of the need for this book and for their numerous ideas, contributions, and suggestions at each stage of the first edition in Spanish, as well as the trust and freedom to move forward with the project.

Turning now to the English version of this book, I would like to thank Rebecca Brennan and J. Michael Ryan for their interest in publishing it with Routledge, and also Christopher Parry for his help with editing, and Barbara Rattner for her confidence in this work and for suggesting its possible destination. I would like to say a special word of thanks to Douglas Andrew Town, who was not only an exquisite translator but also a co-author of this version, adding numerous comments, suggestions, and corrections that have undoubtedly enriched it. Last but not least, the English translation was made possible thanks to the generous financial support of the Programa Sur of the Argentine Ministry of Foreign Affairs.

Finally, these acknowledgments would not be complete without mentioning a few very special individuals: Alejandro Varela, for his support, for his reflections, and for being a good listener. My parents and my sister Liliana, even though we were forced to communicate by phone or by internet without being able to hug one another because of traveling restrictions.

My children, Ezequiel and Tamara, who had the good sense to make me play for a while when they were unable to change the topic of conversation, obsessively limited to a single topic.

And to Virginia Feinmann, because life is more beautiful waking up by your side.

Introduction

Toward the end of 2019, when Alberto Fernández became president of Argentina, alarming news began to arrive from the other side of the planet: a new virus had emerged in the Wuhan region of China. It was causing infections that shared many symptoms with severe acute respiratory syndrome (SARS) originating in China's Guangdong province in November 2002, and the 2009 H1N1 influenza. The world prepared to implement preventive measures as it had done in the past.

However, the speed at which the new virus spread throughout Europe in January 2020 and the alerts issued by the World Health Organization (WHO) made it necessary to rethink political and economic priorities for 2020. These had to be "recalculated" all over the planet. In some cases, the economic and political order itself was called into question.

Governments had to deal with a new phenomenon and one with unforeseeable consequences as the last global pandemic of this magnitude, the "Spanish flu" of 1918–1920, had occurred a century earlier. Therefore, every decision and every new measure was a venture into unknown territory. At the same time, many philosophers and activists had already been expecting an event of this kind – one that would radically change the global order.

In those early days of March and April 2020, some predicted a fundamental shift in international politics. Some, like Slavoj Žižek, believed the COVID-19 pandemic would produce a "Kill Bill" blow to capitalism. Others, like Byung-Chul Han, saw it as an opportunity for governments and multinationals to extend and tighten control of our behavior using the digital panopticon of big data. Some misguided individuals like Giorgio Agamben even imagined that the pandemic was an invention to justify exceptional state measures. However, most observers considered that there would be no major transformations and that we would return in a few months to the same normality we seemed to have abandoned.

DOI: 10.4324/9781003267614-1

Unlike these early and somewhat hasty predictions, this book does not set out to engage in pandemic or post-pandemic futurology. That would be a sterile endeavor, since reality is complex and dynamic, and the future depends largely on what people are willing to do with the phenomena they face. Rather, this book offers a social and political assessment of the events experienced at the planetary level in 2020 and 2021 as a tool for future debates. Naturally, it has been written with the urgency and limitations of the present moment, but I do not believe that this detracts from its validity. It does not take the position of an "analytical outsider," making predictions or ratifying previous assumptions. On the contrary, the idea is to include ourselves as "critical insiders" of the COVID-19 crisis. This crisis is one more terrain in which to consider debates over possible types of community, as well as the shifting power balance in social relations, correlations of forces, and forms of subjectivity.

My aim is to use my decades of previous work on other types of crises or catastrophes (genocide and state crimes) to examine a radically different reality, albeit equally disruptive and badly in need of unpacking.

I am interested in what the pandemic can tell us about how our social relations and representations of reality are being transformed. Or to put it less ambitiously, I am interested in the world of new opportunities that emerges once we are prepared to question our representations of social reality and their role in maintaining unequal power relations.

The occurrence of any catastrophe forces us to question things we normally take for granted. Thus, the COVID-19 crisis makes it possible to imagine different social realities, and this turn may have a more or less profound impact on the social and political processes that shape contemporary subjectivity. It forces us to accept our own limitations but also to recognize our abilities and potentialities. A catastrophe brings us face to face with the possibility that social life could be different from what it is. For example, the product of human labor (including vaccines against a new virus) could be distributed differently in ways that do not involve the growing inequality we accept so unquestioningly and which is, in fact, an insult to human dignity. Our forms of production and consumption (about which we ask ourselves few questions on a daily basis) may not be the only ones imaginable.

The questions of this book are, then, different in nature. What kind of societies faced COVID-19 between January and March 2020? What kind of responses were they able to implement? What nightmares and dreams did the catastrophe evoke, and what potentialities? What kind of experiences has the world gone through since then? What features of these are specific to the Latin American periphery? What particular responses were Argentine society able to offer to this new crisis situation, which was different from and yet comparable to numerous other crises experienced in the last half century? How did these elements come together to build a social representation of this new catastrophe? How can we take stock of the crisis with a view to influencing more general debates about society and the community we wish to live in? How can we draw up a provisional balance sheet of what exists together with what does not exist but can be imagined?

In general, mainstream opinion has failed to realize that despite its biological origin, the pandemic and the measures taken to deal with it are an eminently social phenomenon. Thus, during the first months, medical professionals were assigned the task of providing complex social and political responses beyond the scope of their expertise. They were expected to implement different forms of quarantine, to restrict or prohibit numerous activities including the mobility of the population and the distribution of goods, and even to communicate the new reality to the population as a whole. At the same time, they struggled to rebuild health systems devastated by neoliberalism and to learn about the clinical effects of the virus or the advances in treatments and vaccines to deal with it. Overwhelmed by exceptional events, these medical professionals did the best they could. They took on tasks for which they were unprepared and which required a commitment far beyond any sensible working day. In most cases, they were not even paid for this extra work. The nightly ovations for hospital workers – which of course included these professionals – showed warm appreciation for their efforts but were short-lived and gave way, in many countries, not only to indifference but to mockery, aggression, and even threats. Health professionals had to carry a double burden – the work itself plus the possibility of becoming the bearers of unwelcome news.

Meanwhile, as was to be expected, most physicians proved to be as successful at designing social policies as sociologists would have been at developing vaccines or caring for patients in emergency rooms. No single discipline can solve the challenges of a complex phenomenon such as a pandemic. People often failed to behave according to the healthcare design; the announced "peaks" did not follow the sequence of medical "forecasts" (leaving aside those of mathematicians or computer scientists who could approach the problem in a more scientific and accurate way). As a result, many of those who had prioritized health protection ended up giving in to those who did have a fully sociological, but anti-grass roots, vision of the crisis generated by the pandemic. This fact has never been recognized publicly by most Western governments.

The alternative "solution" – to ignore the pandemic or act as if it did not exist – was explicitly adopted by the governments of the United States and Brazil, and by opposition political groups in several countries, including Argentina. Much more aware of the potential social and political consequences of the COVID-19 crisis, those who advocated this approach aimed first and foremost to safeguard the existing social organization and distribution of income. When the first vaccines began to appear, they considered it essential to protect the patents of the pharmaceutical industry despite enormous state investments and to leave distribution to the market. Consequently, wealthy countries hogged COVID-19 vaccines, leaving a large part of humanity out in the cold as had occurred in previous decades with every other product of human labor.

Despite the magnitude of the catastrophe, the conviction that it was necessary to protect the economic hegemony that had emerged at the end of the Cold War was reinforced by a number of negationist groups. As suffering and hardship increased and conspiracy theories multiplied, many searched for scapegoats on which to unload the hatred and resentment produced by the pandemic. And many governments that initially confronted such behavior without realizing the political challenge it posed ended up backtracking on their original policies and adopting strategies such as "flattening the curve." They accepted high levels of death and affectation as "commonsensical."

This book sets out to enumerate and confront the many different forms of negationism or denial that arose during the pandemic. It explores the potential of catastrophes to transform the status quo in different ways – not in order to predict the future, which is impossible, but to understand what has happened in these last two years and the opportunities the pandemic offers to reset the economy in ways that are both socially just and environmentally sustainable. This may offer the promise of a hope-filled future, which is no small thing.

One of the basic assumptions of this book is that social behavior is rooted in systems of production and consumption and can be analyzed on three different levels: an epistemological level, an emotional-affective level, and an ethical-moral level. These are interrelated but may lead to different representations of social phenomena and so cause us to confront reality differently. Chapter 1 examines the ways in which representations of reality are constructed and the alternative representations that arose in relation to the pandemic in 2020 and 2021. The focus here will be on the epistemological dimension: what it is that makes certain elements of reality (people, actions, events, territories, etc.) visible or invisible and how this determined whether different political responses to the pandemic were perceived as viable or not. It is not a matter of judging this or that government as an outsider or an alienated observer but of recognizing, as protagonists of our own history, what we were or were not capable of doing as a society (this "we" includes but goes way beyond political parties). How did we as a society coordinate our responses to the catastrophe? How did our responses reinforce or undermine the decisions and actions of the government and other political forces and social movements?

Chapters 2 and 3 analyze the emotional-affective and ethical-moral dimensions of behavior. Together they focus on defense mechanisms and, in particular, denial and projection. They argue that shame and guilt are necessary if people are to behave as responsible citizens but that these emotions have been largely erased in neoliberal consumerist societies, which promote selfish individualism and egocentrism. The key question in these chapters is how contemporary subjectivity has evolved over the last half century and how it shaped behavior during the pandemic. The aim is to show how different ways of imagining who we are and how we relate to those around us have a determining effect on how we face a collective catastrophe.

The choice of defense mechanisms is not random. Although many more could be mentioned, I have focused on those that in my opinion played a decisive role in shaping representations and behaviors in 2020 and 2021 with a view to predicting what might happen in future if certain tendencies are reinforced. To do so, I examine some of the political consequences of these emotional and moral elements in other catastrophes throughout history.

Finally, Chapter 4 raises some questions about the ways in which we have dealt with the pandemic and how these may continue to transform social practices and representations of the real in contemporary societies. The focus here is not only on current disputes over representations but also on the potential impact of such representations on social fabric and even our capacity to imagine alternative realities.

In short, we need to resort to the Gramscian concept of "correlation of forces" – the gradual accumulation of political opposition to injustice until it vents in influential sectors of society such as labor unions or popular movements – in order to understand how this pandemic can help challenge neoliberalism and consumerism and the political challenges that this implies. In short, we need to understand that this crisis can also be an opportunity but that it requires the existence of political forces willing to take advantage of it. And that such an opportunity may imply both positive changes and the aggravation of pre-existing trends.

Referring to the efforts of "hegemonic" political forces seeking to defend the status quo, and "counterhegemonic" forces seeking to replace it with a more liberating structure or order, Antonio Gramsci argued:

> These incessant and persistent efforts (since no social formation will ever admit that it has been superseded) form the terrain of the "conjunctural," and it is upon this terrain that the forces of opposition organize [*sic*]. These forces seek to demonstrate that the necessary and sufficient conditions already exist to make possible, and hence imperative, the

accomplishment of certain historical tasks (imperative, because any falling short before an historical duty increases the necessary disorder, and prepares more serious catastrophes). (The demonstration in the last analysis only succeeds and is "true" if it becomes a new reality, if the forces of opposition triumph; in the immediate, it is developed in a series of ideological, religious, philosophical, political, and juridical polemics, whose concreteness can be estimated by the extent to which they are convincing, and shift the previously existing disposition of social forces.)[1]

The key point is that these challenges to the ideological practices that maintain the status quo must be convincing. Hopefully, this book will make a compelling contribution to these "polemics."

For three decades, I have studied the different ways in which genocide could be analyzed as a social practice, one of my aims being to show how it works as a technology of power. To this end, I have shown how different ways of understanding genocide and its effects on social relations in survivor society can influence the correlations of forces within that society. Terror not only transforms the social fabric but also our ability to imagine our future. In this sense, genocide is ultimately instrumental. Indeed, I coined the term "symbolic realization" more than 20 years ago to draw attention to the fact that genocide continues to shape social ties long after the killing has ceased. The aim of genocide is not so much to annihilate the victims as to transform the identity of the survivors, as the creator of the concept of genocide, Rafael Lemkin, observed. Lemkin argued that this transformation depends on the representations a society constructs for itself of what it has experienced, the stories it tells itself about the catastrophe, and the type of impact these stories have on its identity and social practices.

Now, not only is a pandemic not a genocide, it also does not, in itself, constitute a social practice. It is a complex interplay between natural phenomena and social practices, involving a serious disruption of the functioning of society by the natural world. What deserves close sociological scrutiny is how the consequences of a pandemic and, above all, possible community responses to the *social* crisis are represented. This is especially true when a pandemic assumes the dimensions, global impact, and seriousness of the Black Death and the Spanish flu, and now the COVID-19 crisis. A pandemic can produce profound transformations in our identity. As with other catastrophes or significant social events, the COVID-19 crisis will surely disturb our representations of reality and the correlation of forces within society, as well as enabling new behaviors to emerge, both selfish and solidarity-focused.

As this is not a book of futurology, it will make no attempt to predict when the COVID-19 pandemic will end or the total number of global deaths it will leave in its wake. Nor will it try to establish how the mutations and variants of the virus will evolve, how long the vaccination process will take, or whether restrictions will have to be reintroduced for certain activities. Much less will it attempt to predict when the "normality" we knew until the end of 2019 will be restored.

On the contrary, the following pages examine how we have faced the COVID-19 pandemic as a society and the possible consequences of what we were and were not able to achieve. Above all, this book aims to show the many opportunities that open up before us if we are also able to take stock of the pandemic as a society. Many of these opportunities, however, are only possible if we manage to overcome our growing alienation. We need to realize that social action is not something that happens to us, rather, it depends on our ability to make things happen by making responsible decisions. This ability, in turn, is determined by our ability to question our representations of reality on a regular basis and by the stories we tell ourselves about who we are.

Note

1 Antonio Gramsci, *The Modern Prince*, cited in *Selections from the Prison Notebooks of Antonio Gramsci*, edited and translated by Quintin Hoare and Geoffrey Nowell Smith (London: Lawrence & Wishart and New York: International Publishers, 1971), 178.

Bibliography

Agamben, Giorgio, *Where We Are Now. The Epidemic as Politics* (New York and London: Rowman and Littlefield, 2021).

Balsa, Javier, Strategies against the COVID-19 Pandemic and the Crisis of Hegemony, *Notebooks: The Journal for Studies on Power* 1, no. 1 (2021): 96–119, https://doi.org/10.1163/26667185-01010006.

Bauman, Zygmunt, *Postmodern Ethics* (Cambridge: Basil Blackwell, 1993).

Bauman, Zygmung, *Liquid Modernity* (Cambridge: Polity, 2000).

Bauman, Zygmunt, *Community. Seeking Safety in an Insecure World* (Cambridge: Polity, 2001).

Bauman, Zygmunt, *Work, Consumerism and the New Poor* (Berkshire and New York: Open University Press, 2005).

Beck, Ulrich, *Risk Society: Towards a New Modernity* (London and New York: Sage, 1992).

Berger, Peter and Luckmann, Thomas L., *The Social Construction of Reality. A Treatise in the Sociology of Knowledge* (New York: Doubleday, 1966).

Feierstein, Daniel, *Genocide as Social Practice. Reorganizing Society under Nazism and the Argentina Military Juntas* (NJ: Rutgers University Press, 2014).

Freud, Sigmund, "Formulations on the Two Principles of Mental Functioning" (1911), in *The Standard Edition of the Complete Psychological Works of Sigmund Freud* (London: The Hogarth Press and the Institute of Psycho-Analisis, 1958), Volume XII.

Freud, Sigmund, "Beyond the Pleasure Principle" (1920), in *The Standard Edition of the Complete Psychological Works of Sigmund Freud* (London: The Hogarth Press and the Institute of Psycho-Analisis, 1955), Volume XVIII.

Gramsci, Antonio, *Selections from the Prison Notebooks of Antonio Gramsci*, edited and translated by Quintin Hoare and Geoffrey Nowell Smith (London: Lawrence & Wishart and New York: International Publishers, 1971).

Gramsci, Antonio, "Notes for an Introduction and an Approach to the Study of Philosophy and the History of Culture," in *The Gramsci Reader. Selected Writings 1916–1935*, edited by David Forgacs (NY: New York University Press, 2000).

Han, Byung Chul, *Capitalism and the Death Drive* (Cambridge & Medford: Polity Press, 2021).

Žižek, Slavoj, *Pandemic!: COVID-19 Shakes the World* (New York & London: OR Books, 2020).

Žižek, Slavoj, *Pandemic! 2. Chronicles of a Lost Time* (New York: Polity Press, 2021).

1 The dispute over the representations of COVID-19

Before becoming immersed in the debate about different approaches to the pandemic, we need to dispel some common myths about our representations of reality. One widely-held assumption is that these representations are like snapshots of events. The pictures we have may not be perfect but the situations they represent are "out there" in the real world. In the pandemic, this notion has given rise to representations that leave little room for uncertainty – a quality fundamental for understanding new phenomena – or for correcting and updating accepted wisdom. Above all, such forms of representation tend to make certain phenomena invisible because we cannot relate them to our image of ourselves and the world.

Relativism questions this naïve and static way of representing reality by reinterpreting a provocative phrase of the 19th-century philosopher Friedrich Nietzsche. Confronting the positivism of his time, Nietzsche famously said: "There are no facts, only interpretations. (…) But even that is an interpretation."[1]

This relativism has gained a strong foothold since the end of the Cold War and the disappearance of the "old narratives." It has helped spawn the notion that any opinion, however unfounded, should be respected just like any other while forgetting Nietzsche's ironic warning about the subjective nature of interpretations. Indeed, the problem with this sort of relativism is that it becomes impossible to establish an objective reality, however complex, and so act to transform the world effectively.

A good example of relativism can be found in much of today's journalism, where opinions and preconceptions have replaced the fact checking and objective reporting that used to be the bread and butter of the profession. The United States presented by CNN and Fox seems to be two different countries in which completely different events are taking place. The same is true of the Argentina seen on TN and C5N. It is very difficult to understand that these news channels are talking about the same place because we no longer have different views of the same events, which is obviously useful

DOI: 10.4324/9781003267614-2

for forming a critical opinion. Instead we have two conflicting agendas, in which the events themselves differ. With each media outlet pushing different stories, it is as if the events that each of these ignores had never taken place.

Classic journalistic practice, then, has been replaced by an attempt to impose an agenda. This tends to come wrapped in media hype with a profusion of adjectives. The increasing marginalization of specialized journalism is further evidence of the perception that the only thing that matters is "opinion." Science journalism has been particularly hard hit. CNN, for example, cut its entire science, technology, and environment news staff in 2008. Nowadays, the programs with the highest ratings are little more than slanging matches between "panelists" giving their opinions on football, politics, science, economics, health, entertainment, or the trending topic of the day.

Unfortunately, both conservatives, who assume that truth is fixed and unchangeable, and relativists, who see the notion of objective truth as inherently dishonest, are ill-placed to influence reality. This is because they fail to grasp the complex ways in which the mind perceives and represents what happens in our lives and how these representations are linked to social action. There is no easy black-and-white answer to this problem. We do not construct our perceptions automatically from the facts as if we were trying to bring a photograph into focus. But neither can we dispense with objectifiable facts as if reality could be shaped by willpower alone, with no consequences for our lives.

The constructivist approach

The next few pages will look at the ways we represent reality and its connections with purposeful social behavior. Although this topic may seem a bit abstract and theoretical, it is essential to understanding what has happened during the COVID-19 pandemic.

According to Jean Piaget, the Swiss psychologist famous for his work on child development, knowledge arises from the interplay of three basic elements: 1) the real world; 2) how the real world is represented in the mind; and 3) the behavior that arises from these representations and comes up against the real world. Human beings test different hypotheses (i.e. representations) about reality by acting on them in order to see what happens, and in this way they develop knowledge.

This may sound simple but the processes involved are complex. Cognitive elements (what is observed or perceived) depend on previous experiences and the ways in which these are represented in the mind. There is also the problem of how different hypotheses play out in practice.

Emotional elements also play a role. We may find it hard to accept certain interpretations, or we may react to certain passions and fears with psychological defense mechanisms, such as denial, projection, or apathy. Finally, there are moral and ethical considerations. Different interpretations of reality imply different positions with respect to what one is willing to accept or not. Ultimately, it is our fundamental values that guide our behavior and make reality observable or not. As Jayyusi points out, "there are many things that we may look at but not 'see'; things that we 'see' but whose details we do not 'notice,' and things we see or even take minute note of but do not engage."[2]

Cognitive processes and levels of abstraction

According to Piaget, reality is conceptualized through a process of reflection called "awareness," a notion found in classic sociological authors such as Émile Durkheim, Karl Marx, and Max Weber. The "links" between the material world, which exists outside of us, and the categories of thought we use to apprehend it, understand it, and fundamentally, to act in it are established through successive processes of abstraction, some more complex than others.[3]

At the first level we have the conceptualization of *objects*. Now, this may seem a straightforward process, but in fact we need to carry out a series of abstraction operations in order to say, for example, "this is a table." We have to look at the object and, among its thousands of qualities, identify its key attributes – for example, that it is supported by legs and has a surface to place things on. I also have to make sure that these attributes do not belong to any other type of object. For example, chairs also have legs and flat surfaces; however – and this is important – their function is different.[4]

This brings us to the second level – the conceptualization of actions. Here, it is not enough to recognize how an object is used. We also need to know its purpose within a particular environment. In a game of tennis, certain movements allow the racket to hit the ball in different ways. If we perform them correctly, we will be able to put the ball into our opponent's court and even make it very difficult to return the ball. In tennis these strokes are conceptualized as serve, drive, forehand, backhand, smash, lob, etc.

In this way, the strokes end up becoming nouns as if they were objects, but a more complex type of object. In fact, each object is really a coordinated set of actions.

The movements that make each stroke possible in a game of tennis constitute simple actions that involve different objects (the racket, the ball, the court, and the net), the subject who acts, the conditions in which the actions occur, and the relationships that arise between the subject and the objects with which he or she interacts. As any tennis coach knows, a correct handling of these abstractions helps fine-tune players' skills and improve their tennis game.

At a third level of complexity, hypotheses can be established about the meanings and intentions of social behavior. A classic example in sociology is Durkheim's study of the reasons why people commit suicide.[5] This involves hypotheses about intentions, both conscious (for example, the explanation the subject gives for his action in a suicide note) or unconscious (he will only become aware of these if he survives and perhaps enters therapy).

The fourth level is that of *social relations*. Here it is no longer a question of how a subject acts in accordance with conscious or unconscious intentions but the ways in which two or more conscious minds interact over time (also known as "intersubjective determination") and create a common vision and shared frameworks for social action.[6] This level allows us to understand the functioning of groups, the relationships between them, the different levels at which actions are determined, and the long-term structures that drive them. It also explains how collective motivations and representations are constructed, as well as the way in which representations sedimented in the past impose limits on the imaginative possibilities of the present and how these can be challenged.

For example, economic oppression may take many forms: slavery, low wages, denial of equal opportunities, sexual discrimination, etc. In each case, one group of people is unfairly enjoying the fruits of another group's labor. But this appropriation can be concealed or justified as an act of divine providence or a "natural" result of market laws. In very different contexts, thinkers such as Marx and Heidegger used the concept of "alienation" to describe such distorted representations of social reality.

All this may seem very theoretical and far removed from the problem of the pandemic. However, as we will see, it will provide important tools to help us think about our ability to respond as a society to the coronavirus pandemic.

Disputes about the forms of representation of COVID-19

The biological level

The first representations to appear during a pandemic are biological. Doctors and scientists attempt to explain the social changes brought about by the new virus or new bacteria. The virus responsible for the current pandemic emerged in the city of Wuhan, China, in 2019 and was unknown before it migrated to humans. Christened SARS-CoV-2, it is a coronavirus, so-called because of its crown-like appearance under the microscope. It causes the respiratory disease known as coronavirus disease 2019 (COVID-19).

The name SARS-CoV-2 was chosen because the virus is genetically related to the coronavirus responsible for the outbreak of severe acute respiratory syndrome (SARS) in 2002. Now, it is important to remember that contrary to what some schools of logic believe, knowledge tends to progress by developing good analogies. In this case, it was an analogy with the 2002 SARS virus that allowed us to form a preliminary representation of the SARS-2 virus, even though the two are very different. Indeed, despite being the same type of virus (coronavirus) and causing the type of syndrome (severe acute respiratory syndrome), it is now becoming clear that SARS-2 creates different complications than the original SARS.

Gradually, more has become known about this new SARS-CoV-2 virus. However, initially the greatest concern was that no-one knew precisely how the infection was spread, what kind of problems it caused, or how lethal it might be. The analogy with SARS was not sufficient to answer these questions, due to the enormous variability shown by coronaviruses, with many different strains and variants.

For example, just as it was being confirmed that the SARS-CoV-2 virus produced severe acute respiratory syndrome, it was also found to produce inflammation of the liver, heart, kidneys, and brain in some patients. Attributed to a "cytokine storm," this inflammation quickly led to multiorgan failure, especially among diabetics and obese patients, among others. There were no known successful treatments for this new virus or the different forms the illness could take, and little was known about the sequelae it might leave. In fact we still know very little about its long-term aftereffects.

Another incognita is how long immunity lasts after a SARS-CoV-2 infection. An article published in *Nature* on May 26, 2021 suggests that people who recover from *mild* COVID-19 will continue to produce antibodies for decades.[7] However, this remains to be seen, as we have experienced reinfections with different COVID-19 variants like alpha, beta, gamma, lambda, delta, or omicron during 2021 and 2022. Nor is there much information on possible mutations and the effectiveness of naturally acquired immunity to different variants and strains of the virus.

Alarm bells went off in the medical community and the World Health Organization (WHO) at the beginning of 2020 after it was found that mortality rates for COVID-19 are significantly higher than for respiratory diseases such as influenza. Rapid and drastic action was needed to prevent the global spread of the virus and the saturation of health systems. It was then that the second analogy arose, linked more to the likely *social* effects of the virus: the analogy with the so-called Spanish flu of 1918–1920. This pandemic, the deadliest in modern history, not only killed an estimated 20 to

50 million people worldwide but it came in waves – the second more lethal than the first – which made it very difficult to combat.

With this analogy we can see how more complex levels of abstraction start to become involved: actions, intentions, associated effects, coordination of public policies, social responses, and geopolitical relations, the feasibility or unfeasibility of the policies implemented, and their economic consequences.

On the biological level of analysis, then, we had a new virus capable of killing or severely disabling the elderly and those suffering from diabetes, obesity, and/or respiratory and cardiovascular diseases, among others. Moreover, there was no successful treatment or vaccine and no information about long-term outcomes for those who had recovered from the virus, how long their acquired immunity might last naturally, how many strains it might protect them against, or what effects future mutations of the virus might have.

Although these questions have not been fully answered by the research published to date, the lack of knowledge and uncertainty was much greater in February or March 2020. At that time it was not even known how the virus spread. It was not until the second half of 2020 that SARS-CoV-2 was shown to be spread by airborne transmission – although the WHO had downplayed earlier evidence of this, thus repeating the mistake it had made with regard to measles. The strongest work to date confirms that the virus is spread by aerosols – i.e. liquid droplets suspended in the atmosphere.[8] It also seems clear that asymptomatic people are contagious. The viral load carried by an infected person (and this can be very high even in asymptomatic people) can affect the contagiousness and the severity of the illness, although the latter point is disputed.[9]

Social behavior

The nature of representations of the pandemic becomes more complex when we include the dimension of social and political responses to the initial events. In this sense, different representations of the pandemic were determined not only by cognitive but by emotional and moral factors related to different political worldviews and material interests. The problem of how to deal with this new threat to human life began to divide governments and populations.

In late 2019, responses to the emergence of COVID-19 were not the same across the globe. In terms of epistemological and moral assumptions, the clearest difference was that of separating Western and Asian countries, both at the level of government and society. Countries such as China, South Korea, Singapore, Vietnam, and Thailand quickly tried to contain the virus through a so-called elimination strategy. These included medieval-style quarantines and total blockades of affected areas for as long as necessary in order to contain the spread of disease; border controls; intensive contact tracing; and traceability and isolation policies (in many cases using geolocation technologies), among others.

Many Western countries, on the other hand, espoused a strategy of "herd immunity." This was initially the case in Sweden, the United Kingdom, the United States, and Brazil. Herd immunity is the indirect protection from an infectious disease that happens when a population is immune either through vaccination or immunity developed through previous infection.

In other words, they decided to let the virus spread through the population until most people had been infected and could no longer pass on the illness to the unprotected. The rationale for this decision was that lockdowns would seriously damage the economy. It was not until the death toll continued to rise in Germany, the Netherlands, the United States, and Switzerland and the hospital system had reached breaking point in countries like Spain, Italy, the United Kingdom, Belgium, and France that preventive measures were introduced. By then, intensive care units were collapsing due to the number of severe cases of coronavirus, making it impossible to attend to other serious conditions, such as accidents, heart attacks, or stroke. Thus, changing the initial strategy of "herd immunity" for one of mitigation, or "flattening the curve," also sought to prevent additional non-COVID-related deaths.

With regard to the economy, numerous studies have shown that during the 1918–1920 Spanish flu pandemic, virus eradication policies not only resulted in a significantly lower loss of lives but also allowed for a faster economic recovery. In fact, death rates were around 50 percent lower in US cities that implemented virus eradication policies earlier and more aggressively.[10] These measures, which included closing schools and banning public gatherings, as well as mandatory quarantines, face masks, and social distancing, also allowed for faster economic recovery when they were not relaxed too early.[11,12]

Despite this evidence from an earlier pandemic, most Western nations did not change their approach. This took a heavy toll in terms of lives (millions of deaths due to COVID-19), while allowing the virus to permanently mutate into more contagious and/or more lethal variants like alpha, gamma, lambda, delta, or omicron variants as the most prevalent during 2021. Future mutations of the virus may become resistant to existing vaccines, constituting a danger even for societies that have managed to eradicate or control the virus.

Creating immunity through different social behaviors

Ever since the pandemic began, Roberto Etchenique, an Argentine researcher at the National Council for Scientific and Technical Research (CONICET) has been trying to understand it from a variety of perspectives. Although a chemist, he has investigated the sociological dimension and demonstrated the value of transdisciplinary approaches to complex phenomena.[13] Partly as a joke but with a notable effect on understanding the forms of representation that occurred in several European countries, Etchenique coined the expression "scared shitless immunity."[14] This concept sought to explain why mitigation strategies worked even though the health systems in countries like Italy or Spain were collapsing. According to Etchenique, a large part of the population of these countries stayed at home, terrified that they would not be admitted to hospital if they developed COVID-19. This "scared shitless immunity" was very different from the "herd immunity" mentioned earlier.

Mathematical modeling has been used in many countries to predict the spread of the virus. In Argentina, Rodrigo Castro, Ernesto Kofman, Rodrigo Quiroga, and Guillermo "Willy" Durán, as well as Etchenique himself, all developed computer simulations to estimate the effect of different interventions.[15] A significant drop in the number of cases among vulnerable and high risk groups eventually brought the hospital situation under control. More recently, R0 and Rt rates have become common terms in the media as Rt rates have dropped below 1.0. R0 (pronounced "R-naught") refers to how many people will catch the disease from a single infected person. Rt refers to the actual reproduction rate of the virus at a particular point in time. An Rt of 1.0 indicates that a disease is endemic and will persist over time. An Rt of more than 1.0 means the infection is spreading fast, while an Rt of less than 1.0 means it is not spreading and – if this situation persists – the virus will eventually die out.

However, the virus was never eliminated in those countries that did not adopt an elimination strategy from day one. The decline in Rt rates has depended until now on large swathes of the population remaining frightened enough to restrict their movements and social contacts. Unfortunately, as soon as the situation improves and the healthcare system starts to return to normal, people lower their guard. As the virus begins to spread again, this creates a second or third "wave" of infection as experienced in most Western countries of the northern hemisphere in late fall and early winter of 2020. In contrast, countries that initially chose to suppress the virus and contain the few cases that did occur have not experienced this phenomenon. Since people in many Western countries were no longer "scared shitless" during the second and third waves because they had come to terms with the pandemic, these waves tended to be more severe than the first one in terms of number of infections and number of deaths.

Something worth noting is that the decisive element of the representations that influenced social behaviors at the beginning was an emotion: fear. This emotional response was much more effective than a rational analysis of the advantages of this or that strategy. People decided to stay at home not because they were convinced about their government's policy for dealing with the pandemic but because television images showed hospitals on the verge of collapse. Once fears subsided – because the pandemic had become normalized, the health situation was improving, and other needs were pressing – people relaxed their precautions and a second wave occurred. In countries such as Austria, Germany, and Switzerland, this resulted in significantly more deaths than during the first wave.

Nevertheless, it is also true that some Western countries opted in the early days of the current coronavirus pandemic for a containment strategy, with results similar to those in Asian countries. This was the case of Norway, Finland, Australia, and New Zealand, among others during 2020 and 2021, and this point is important because it shows that cultures are not watertight compartments. It also shows that exploring different representations of reality can allow us to engage in significantly different social actions and inter-actions that are not determined beforehand. This is perhaps the only way to transform our reality, including the economic and social consequences of the pandemic.

Economist Branko Milanović has analyzed what makes different strate-gies acceptable or not in different societies in terms of the way different cultures relate to time. These relationships can be disputed and can undergo change, but it seems that changes may take longer than our contemporary anxiety is prepared to wait.[16]

Sigmund Freud and Donald Winnicott, among others, have shown the importance of delayed gratification and impulse control for personality development.[17] A healthy adult personality is characterized by the ability to postpone gratification until it is realistic or acceptable. People willing and able to make temporary sacrifices are more successful in their studies, careers, relationships, health, finances, and most other areas of life.

Unfortunately, we live in a time of constantly accelerating economic cycles and market globalization. This makes us increasingly anxious to consume goods and services, especially in Western societies. The way rep-resentations change in such a context, where consumers find it increasingly difficult to postpone gratification, may explain why so many Western socie-ties failed in the fight against the coronavirus.

Milanović claims that the modern tendency to "live the moment" meant that Western subjectivities often lacked the patience to allow different COVID-19 containment measures to take effect.[18] This would explain how social factors gave rise to differences in the way the crisis was managed in different Western countries and why these measures often failed. Even in the few cases where restrictions were partly offset by social and economic programs, they became difficult to sustain over time. After a few days or weeks of restrictions, small violations of the rules began to appear and these increased each day with virtually no penalties. The reluctance of Western governments to demand and enforce compliance was fundamental to understanding why quarantines failed and the virus became uncontainable.

However, this state of affairs is not inevitable and we do not need to resign ourselves to the situation generated by the pandemic. On the contrary, we should include our inability or unwillingness to act as an input in the dispute over representations and their ability to influence social actions.

The pandemic in Latin America

Latin America was at a significant disadvantage when it came to dealing with the pandemic. Its fragile social structure made any "herd" strategy particularly dangerous, but it was also difficult to implement the contact tracing used in Asia, Australia, and New Zealand. These difficulties were linked both to social relationships and structural variables that shape social ties in each country (i.e. types of economy and accumulation models), as well as the specific ways in which subjectivity has developed in the region. As part of the "Western world," Latin America shows the same impatience and the same demand for instant results as mentioned earlier. However, it has its own idiosyncrasies and – even if it sometimes shows an interesting potential for change – it is more prone to conflict than cooperation.[19]

Latin America is one of the most unequal regions on the planet, with extremely high levels of poverty and overcrowding in large cities. These include Mexico City; Bogota, Cali, and Medellin; Quito and Guayaquil; La Paz; Lima; Sao Paulo and Rio de Janeiro; Buenos Aires, Rosario, and Cordoba; and Santiago de Chile, among others. Most workers earn their livelihoods in the informal economy without proper integration into the social protection system. Consequently, millions of people in Latin America have difficulties in accessing clean water, food, housing, and state care. In addition health systems in the region have been ravaged by decades of economic "adjustments."

As a result, the region's only hope was to try to contain the outbreak very early, before it spread to the poorest neighborhoods, where it would be impossible to implement restrictions or effective contact tracing. The one factor the region had in its favor among a host of negative ones was the fact that the pandemic had started in distant China before spreading to Europe. It only began to reach Latin America after a delay of one to two months. But by then the public health risk was clear.

It was obvious that any herd strategy in Latin America would lead to a serious collapse of the entire health system within days or weeks. The only viable strategy in January and February 2020 (when virus data were beginning to be known) was early intervention, which meant closing borders, strict controls on travelers coming from abroad, and a short but very strict quarantine to isolate cases that had already entered the country. Unfortunately, it is precisely during these two months that international tourism arrivals reach their peak in the southern hemisphere due to the summer season.

Another problem that made it difficult for Latin American countries to respond effectively to the pandemic was the absence of the state in poor urban neighborhoods and remote rural areas. To reach these areas required close cooperation between the state and organizations that generally confront or oppose the *status quo* but can go where the state does not. These include soup kitchens, churches, movements that bring together the unemployed or informal workers, *piqueteros*, rural movements linked to land seizures or alternative projects, and indigenous organizations.

Many countries in the region also have insurgent movements in more or less open conflict with state security forces, as well as criminal organizations linked to drug trafficking and other illegal activities. Either of these may control territories the state cannot reach.[20] However, if these uniquely complex forms of territorial control constituted a problem for fighting the pandemic, the pandemic also offered a stimulus and an opportunity to rethink the political structures of the region. At the very least, a concerted management of the pandemic by state and non-state networks would have altered established notions (or "representations") of community, including the inclusion or exclusion of certain groups.

In the event, most Latin American governments failed to take into account the socio-economic, health, urban, and territorial problems of the region, much less the opportunity to begin tackling these. Instead of choosing the only realistic option – suppressing the virus, preferably before it spread – they decided to "flatten the curve" in an attempt to achieve herd immunity.

In some countries, such as Argentina, this strategy was accompanied by serious attempts to strengthen the health system as quickly as possible in order to prevent the collapse observed in some European countries. Extra beds and respirators were added in public hospitals that were under-resourced – as in many developed countries – due to policies of economic adjustment. One of the main problems in strengthening health care systems was the time needed to train enough doctors, nurses, and specialists to deal with the pandemic at the hospital level. This problem proved difficult to overcome even when governments were prepared to invest in healthcare.

The challenges and responses in Argentina

Spanish Silicon Valley engineer Tomás Pueyo has been a good analyst of this pandemic since his first publications appeared in February and March

2020. Although he does not come from the field of epidemiology, his article "The hammer and the dance" had a great impact as it clearly explained two necessary stages in the response to the pandemic.[21] The *hammer* (very strict restrictions on the movement of people) is essential to prevent or drastically reduce the spread of the virus. This move was thwarted in most of Latin America by a massive influx of people from countries with high COVID-19 infection rates who were not properly isolated on their return. After this first stage, it is necessary to move on to the *dance*: tracing and isolating cases and contacts to prevent new waves of COVID-19 and a new cycle of lockdowns (i.e. a new *hammer*).

During the *hammer* stage, Latin America was forced to resort to decisions that were different from those applied in the rest of the world. Overcrowding and inequality in the region's large urban areas made it impossible to impose strict quarantines in poorer neighborhoods. Since the virus was spread by travelers returning from abroad, mass organizations and academics in Argentina suggested implementing so-called "community quarantines" within working class areas, particularly in the industrial belts surrounding large cities. These would allow people to circulate freely within their own neighborhood but would isolate them from the rest of the urban area. The idea was to delay the arrival of the virus in each neighborhood for as long as possible.

It is worth emphasizing that this was an "emergency response" since it was inconceivable that communities could be kept in isolation for more than two or three consecutive weeks. But the initiative might buy time to develop other strategies. In fact, the strategy of community quarantines proved to be successful in Argentina. It was not until the last week in April that the virus entered Villa 31, the slum area closer to the city center of Buenos Aires, and shortly after that, Villa 1-11-14 and Villa 21-24. It took another month to reach the more remote slums or those less well connected with the city center of Buenos Aires. The virus did not reach these neighborhoods until the end of May and the beginning of June 2020, two to three months after the pandemic began in the country.

Unfortunately, lockdown ended up being the only measure deployed. The Argentine government refused to consider other alternatives, such as delegating decision-making to local health systems or using local organizations for contact tracing, even though these had proved successful in large metropolitan Argentine areas like Rosario and Córdoba. Its repeated dismissal of these approaches was responsible for some of the most important mistakes in health management at the national level.

The failure of the *hammer* stage in the Buenos Aires Metropolitan Area, Río Negro, and Chaco made it difficult to appreciate the success of this strategy in the rest of Argentina. The almost exclusive focus on Buenos

Aires that characterizes Argentine provincial life – since most of the media are based in the nation's capital – brought pessimism to the rest of the country. This played a very negative role when the virus began to spread across the country, making it impossible to implement *hammers* when they became necessary. Such was the case in Santa Fe, Rosario, Córdoba, Mar del Plata, Mendoza, Salta, and Jujuy between July and August 2020. The result was even higher rates of infection and death compared to those previously experienced in the Buenos Aires Metropolitan Area.

Thus, the predominant representation of attempts to contain the pandemic gradually became one of *inefficiency*. Argentina ended up with an infection rate similar to the countries that had implemented very few restrictions (Brazil or the United States, for example). The success achieved in most of the country between April and August 2020 counted for nothing as the virus spread from the Buenos Aires Metropolitan Area to the rest of the country. This played an important role in cognitive, emotional, and ethical-moral terms in undermining the precautionary principle in collective representations of the COVID-19 pandemic. On the contrary, a sense of the uselessness of the precautionary measures was consolidated in the Argentine government and the Argentina media from mid-2021.[22] This image of inefficiency was so powerful that it not only took hold in the most individualistic and conservative sectors of society, but also in many areas of the government and its supporters.

But Argentina's problem was not solely or even chiefly the failure of the *hammer* stage. The country faced severe limitations at the *dance* stage. Unlike Asian and Australasian countries, such as South Korea, Singapore, Hong Kong, Taiwan, Australia, or New Zealand, Latin America did not have the technological, political, or social resources to implement this stage successfully. In Asian countries, the relative success of tracking was due to the traceability of people via digital systems, and state persecution and punishment of offenders. Thus, government measures controlling and documenting people's movements and social encounters were strictly complied with. This was inconceivable in Argentina. Argentina lacks the large-scale digital surveillance systems, internet connections, and databases needed to produce and process such information. In any case, these would hardly be viable within poor neighborhoods, some of them without electricity. Moreover, such a massive invasion of privacy runs counter to the individualistic, rebellious tendencies of the urban middle classes and a healthy distrust of surveillance by society as a whole. The Argentine intelligence services have a long history of illegal spying for political gain, including a systematic use of blackmail.

The problem, then, was to create a specifically Argentine *dance* stage that might perhaps serve as an example, like community quarantines, for other countries in the region. No Latin American country succeeded in adapting test-trace-isolate (TTI) programs to take account of the specific strengths and weaknesses of Latin American societies. Strengths included the active role of local grass-roots organizations in different parts of the country (e.g. their political involvement and organizational capacity) and the creativity of Argentine scientific teams. Weaknesses included geolocation difficulties, overcrowded housing, differences in local customs and social networks, as well as the limited outreach of the state, all of which would have required special compensatory measures.

The ASPI Argentine proposal (Selective, Planned, and Intermittent Isolations)

Faced with a rapid increase in the number of infections and deaths throughout the country, most Argentine politicians saw no alternative but to continue with the nationwide lockdown. However, in August 2020 a group of human rights organizations, trade unions, health personnel, and scientists from different fields presented a better proposal. It was known as ASPI (Selective, Planned, and Intermittent Isolation), to distinguish it from the earlier ASPO (Obligatory Preventive Social Isolation) which had failed to isolate or prevent and was obligatory in name only.[23]

Rodrigo Castro, an Argentine expert in computational simulation, and his team had been developing ASPI together with other experts in April 2020. This new approach took account of the need to forecast trends using available epidemiological data in order to design more precise intervention measures, including short, planned lockdowns. In April 2020, a preliminary version had been presented in an internal technical report for the Secretariat of Scientific and Technological Coordination of the Ministry of Science, Technology, and Innovation, and sent to the Office of the National President. It received no response.

The computer simulations developed by Castro's team, and improved on by Ernesto Kofman, a researcher from the National Scientific and Technical Research Council (CONICET) and the National University of Rosario, estimated the spread of the virus in each province over the coming weeks. They included variables such as activities transmitting the virus (based on epidemiological surveys), geographical and/or social sectors in which these occur, implementation of risk reduction and healthcare campaigns, and strengthening of prevention and control measures, among others. One important factor considered by ASPI was the dispute over social representations. The short lockdowns mentioned earlier were to be accompanied by a vigorous harm-reduction campaign informing the public about healthcare policies and how the virus is spread, including the recently confirmed aerosol (airborne) transmission of the disease. Social scientists were brought in to design measures that were ultimately much more sociological than biological.

For policies to be successful, it was not enough to understand the behavior of the virus. It was also necessary to understand how humans respond to disasters and other traumatic events in order to promote awareness and self-control among the population, which is the only way to transform behavior. The initiative was designed to replace massive and politically unfeasible lockdowns with closures that would be short (ten to twenty days), selective (in certain places or only for certain activities), and planned (so that the population would know in advance when they would begin and end). These sporadic closures were expected to produce a drastic reduction in the rate of propagation and would provide data for future computer simulations. Thus, a "new normality" could be established based on routines of closures and openings that the population as a whole could integrate into their daily lives. Precise and timely interventions would reduce the economic cost of fighting the pandemic as well as improving health outcomes. Publishing computer simulations of the number of lives that could be saved *before* each intervention took place would help bring on board sectors of society so far reluctant to accept more restrictions.

Unfortunately, the proposal was never implemented despite numerous consultations with national government and expressions of support from various provinces, departments, and cities throughout 2020 and the first half of 2021.

The timeline of events described so far is essential to understand why large masses of the population succumbed to different forms of denial. The first wave of the pandemic in Argentina (March through September 2020) ended in a way contrary to what had been expected. The initial response had been a willingness to put health before economics under the leadership of a recently elected and popular president, supported by a responsible opposition. A battery of economic containment measures, including tax cuts, tax deferrals, and a wealth tax were introduced to distribute the cost of the crisis more fairly. The first wave ended with a widespread conviction that it was not possible to do anything about the virus and that it was better to let things take their course and wait for one of the vaccines still being tested.

This gradual refocusing of policies went hand in hand with the growth and consolidation of denial. Denial as a universal psychological response to catastrophes has no political color. In October and November 2020, it helped produce the final abandonment of the precautionary principle and bring the death toll to several tens of thousands.

The social construction of reality and its effects on political decisions

Beyond health measures and economic strategies to mitigate lockdown, the main focus was the field of representations. The initial strategy of suppressing the virus, making life and health the priorities, gradually lost ground because of various government errors and decisions.

Representations of the pandemic were rooted in existing social and epistemic attitudes and in political divisions. An example of this was the situation of the returnees. A strict control of a few thousand middle or upper class individuals returning from trips abroad seemed "unthinkable," even though it was clearly essential to the policy of suppressing the virus. The idea that travelers would observe a strict, 14-day quarantine simply because they had signed a commitment to do so on arrival at the airport was completely naïve and unreal.

As mentioned earlier, the decision to send returnees from abroad to hotels was never complied with on a large scale in many Western countries. Moreover, it was made when tens of thousands of people had already entered those countries from the most infected regions of the world. A large percentage had met with relatives and friends and had moved freely around the cities, shopping for food and personal hygiene products or paying their bills. The same happened later, when the arrival of the alpha, gamma, lambda, delta, and omicron variants triggered new waves of the pandemic. Without roadblocks and checkpoints like those that China imposed around the virus-stricken city of Wuhan, it was inevitable that the pandemic would spread from the main cities to the whole country in most of the world.

As the pandemic spread, it became increasingly difficult for the population to focus on the positive results of lockdowns. Economic assistance was slow and designed just for a time of emergency. It was not enough to sustain millions of people over a period of months. People began to disobey restrictions on businesses and other activities. There was no proposal to extend aid to other social sectors or increase benefits, since the cost would have been unfeasible without a profound change in the country's income structure.

Another factor that impacted greatly on public representations of the pandemic was the permanent ridiculing in the press and on radio and television of the "exaggerated" nature of the lockdown measures. Many radio and television programs began by announcing: "This is day X of quarantine," which only worsened anxiety among the population and made it harder to accept the need to postpone gratification.

This played a crucial role in undermining the precautionary principle. Similarly, most of the media focused on the serious economic damage caused by the COVID-19 pandemic (thus normalizing existing forms of income distribution).

The corporatist approach: each man for himself

Together these factors helped accentuate negative reactions to lockdown. Society gradually embraced various forms of denial, confusing health restrictions meant for the good of the society with a limitation of rights or political persecution from a different era. As the debate began focusing on specific activities (for example, whether or not to authorize jogging in the city's parks or workplace safety standards for hairdressing salons), it ended up strengthening the dichotomy of "authoritarianism versus freedom" in people's minds. Thus, governments became seen as "authorizers" or "repressors" and the community as a "victim" of this "arbitrary" state power. Thus, various economic sectors, including nightclubs and sex workers, held public demonstrations (which were not allowed because of social distancing) to demand concessions.

The "culture of fear" communicated by the media that kept Europe's population at home during the first wave of the pandemic never took hold of Latin American societies to the same extent.[24] This shows that it is social representations (not objective data) that determine behavior. The number of deaths in Argentina, Bolivia, Brazil, Chile, Colombia, Ecuador, Mexico, and Peru were equal to or even higher than those in Italy or Spain in proportion to population, but this fact was not made visible in social representations. Instead, the first wave of the pandemic was processed emotionally in terms of partisan debates about civil rights, worries about a possible "infectatorship," and attempts by the media and radical sectors of the new right to delegitimize the containment efforts.

At the same time, many people wavered between denial and acceptance. This is a normal disaster response and one that makes it difficult for individuals to identify the danger to themselves or their loved ones. Not even the collapse of the health system in some countries or districts achieved visibility. The desperate entreaties of health professionals failed to capture the attention of the media, the political authorities, or the Argentine population.

An inability to interpret these debates as different representations of reality widened the gap between medical and scientific advice and public health policies. Thus, for example, the city of Buenos Aires defied a national presidential decree issued on April 16, 2021 to close schools during the second wave of the pandemic. To make matters worse, the Argentine Supreme Court ruled in favor of the city's government, stating that regional governments could "prioritize the opening and resumption of face-to-face classes," which undercut the possibility of a centralized response to the pandemic.

For the most part, however, Latin America countries – despite sharing the same subjective approach to the pandemic – were in a much worse position objectively to deal with its consequences. This contradiction between subjective perceptions and objective realities meant that most of Latin America experienced one of the highest death rates per million inhabitants on the planet.

Notes

1 Friedrich Nietzsche, Der Wille zur Macht. Eine Auslegung alles Geschehens, edited by Max Brahn (Leipzig: Alfred Kröner Verlag, 1917), t. III, § 276, available online at: www.gutenberg.org/files/60360/60360-h/60360-h.htm. The German philosopher's phrase was created in another context. Although it has been popularized as a phrase to legitimize the most extreme subjectivism, this does not follow in any way from the thought of the author himself. Nietzsche does not intend to legitimize subjectivism, but problematizes the dispute against the positivism of his time if we follow his train of thought. In it, to the famous phrase: "Facts is precisely what there are not, there are only interpretations," he goes on to add: "Everything is subjective, you say. But even that is an interpretation. The subject is not something given, it is something added, invented and projected behind what there is. Is it finally necessary to suppose an interpreter behind the interpretation? Even that is invention, a hypothesis. If the word 'knowledge' had any meaning, the world would be 'knowable'. But the world is also interpretable in another way, having not one but innumerable meanings behind it. Perspectivism" (ibid.).

2 Lena Jayyusi, "The Reflexive Nexus: Photo-Practice and Natural History," *Continuum: The Australian Journal of Media & Cultural Studies* 6, no. 2 (1993): 25–52, https:doi.org/10.1080/10304319309359397.

3 This was richly analyzed by Jean Piaget in numerous works, including *The Grasp of Consciousness: Action and concept in the young child* (London: Routledge and Kegan Paul, 1977) [*La prise de conscience* (1974)], and, in collaboration with Rolando García, *Psychogenesis and the History of Science* (New York: Columbia University Press, 1989) *Psychogenèse et histoire des sciences* (1983). Also in Jean Piaget, *The Equilibration of Cognitive Structures: The Central Problem of Intellectual Development* (Chicago: University of Chicago Press, 1985) [*L'equilibration des structures cognitives* (1975), previously translated as *The development of thought: Equilibration of cognitive structures* (1977)]. For Piaget, cognitive levels related to the processes of representation are determined by the ways of abstracting and "thematizing" the realities with which one interacts, that is to say that abstractions construct previous abstractions that are already objectivized as objects of knowledge (this is what Piaget calls "thematization" and shows the richness and complexity of the process).

4 As Eleanor Rosch points out in "Principles of Categorization" (1978): "What attributes will be perceived given the ability to perceive them is undoubtedly determined by many factors having to do with the *functional* needs of the knower interacting with the physical and social environment" (emphasis added). https://commonweb.unifr.ch/artsdean/pub/gestens/f/as/files/4610/9778_083247.pdf.

5 The best known work on the subject is that of Émile Durkheim, *Le Suicide: Étude de sociologie* [1897], published in English in 1952 by Routledge & Kegan Paul as *Suicide: A Study in Sociology*. It is a classic example of sociological research for anyone entering the discipline.

6 See the classic work by Maurice Halbwachs, *The Social Frameworks of Memory* (Les cadres sociaux de la mémoire, 1925).

7 Ewen Callaway, "Had COVID? You'll Probably Make Antibodies for a Lifetime," May 26, 2021, https://www.nature.com/articles/d41586-021-01442 -9.

8 See EU Science Hub. COVID-19: "How a Better Understanding of Airborne Transmission is the Key to Break the Chain of Infection," https://ec.europa.eu /jrc/en/news/covid-19-how-better-understanding-airborne-transmission-key -break-chain-infection.

9 On the transmission by asymptomatic persons and the role of viral load, see Michael A. Johansson, Talia M. Quandelacy, Sarah Kada, Pragati Venkata Prasad, Molly Steele, John T. Brooks, Rachel B. Slayton, Matthew Biggerstaff, and Jay C. Butler, "SARS-CoV-2 Transmission from People without COVID-19 Symptoms," *JAMA Network Open* 4, no. 1 (2021): e2035057, https://jamanet-work.com/journals/jamanetworkopen/fullarticle/2774707.

10 Nina Strochlic and Andriley D. Champine, "How Some Cities 'Flattened the Curve' during the 1918 Flu Pandemic," *National Geographic*, September 2020, https://www.nationalgeographic.com/history/article/how-cities-flattened-curve -1918-spanish-flu-pandemic-coronavirus.

11 Sergio Correia, Stephan Luck, and Emil Verner, "Pandemics Depress the Economy, Public Health Interventions Do Not: Evidence from the 1918 Flu" (June 5, 2020), Available at SSRN: https://ssrn.com/abstract=3561560 or http:// dx.doi.org/10.2139/ssrn.3561560.

12 See Michael G. Baker, Nick Wilson, and Tony Blakely, "Elimination Could Be the Optimal Response Strategy for Covid-19 and Other Emerging Pandemic Diseases," *BMJ* 371 (2020): 1–4; Miquel Oliu-Barton, Bary S.R. Pradelski, Philippe Aghion, Patrick Artus, Ilona Kickbusch, Jeffrey V. Lazarus, Devi Sridhar, and Samantha Vanderslott, "SARS-Cov-2 Elimination, not Mitigation, Creates Best Outcomes for Health, the Economy, and Civil Liberties," *The Lancet* 397 (2021): 2234–2236, https://doi.org/10.1016/S0140-6736(21)00978- 8. For the cost of sustaining mitigation strategies due to the high level of in-hospital COVID-19 mortality, see also Richard A. Armstrong, Andrew D. Kane, Emira Kursumovic, Fiona C. Oglesby, and Tim M. Cook, "Mortality in Patients Admitted to Intensive Care with COVID-19: An Updated Systematic Review and Meta-Analysis of Observational Studies," *Anaesthesia* 76 (2021): 537–548, https://doi.org/10.1111/anae.15425.

13 On the impossibility of approaching complex phenomena without reformulating the ways of doing science and the construction of inter- and transdisciplinary approaches, see Rolando García, *Sistemas complejos. Conceptos, método y fundamentación epistemológica de la investigación interdisciplinaria* (Barcelona: Gedisa, 2006).

14 Etchenique created this concept almost as a joke in Argentine transdisciplinary working groups on the subject. It was taken up again in some newspapers, for example, La Capital, https://www.lacapital.com.ar/pandemia/que-es-la-inmu-nidad-cagazo-y-que-puede-frenar-la-propagacion-del-coronavirus-n2607639 .html; El Cohete a la Luna, https://www.elcohetealaluna.com/la-inmunidad-de

-cagazo-no-llega-sola/; and Infobae, https://www.infobae.com/salud/2020/08/30/que-es-la-inmunidad-del-susto-la-provocadora-hipotesis-de-un-cientifico-del-conicet/, among others. A more systematic development of this concept is needed since it explains convincingly how fear-induced behaviors that created immunity disappeared as soon as the fear behind them ceased to be dominant.

15 See, for example, the project led by Guillermo Durán: "Mathematical-computational tools for the intelligent control of isolation levels in each municipality of the conurbation of the province of Buenos Aires," and the project led by Rodrigo Castro: "Projection of trends and evaluation of intervention scenarios for the COVID-19 epidemic in Argentina through modeling and computational simulation," both funded by the Ministry of Science, Technology, and Productive Innovation. Both researchers are funded by CONICET and based at the Faculty of Exact and Natural Sciences of the University of Buenos Aires (UBA). Guillermo Durán also directs the project "Development of optimization tools, statistics and data science for the management, monitoring and evaluation of public policies," of the Research and Development Projects in Strategic Areas (PIDAE) program of the UBA. For Rodrigo Quiroga, see Germán Soldano, Juan Fraire, Jorge Finochietto, and Rodrigo Quiroga, "On the Effectiveness of Digital Contact Tracing and Contact Prevention under Varying COVID-19 Infection Detection Rates," preprint of an article to be published in *The Lancet. Infectious Diseases*, kindly provided by the author.

16 See Branko Milanović, "Impatience: A Deep Cause of Western Failure in Handling the Pandemic?" December 15, 2020, https://www.globalpolicyjournal.com/blog/15/12/2020/impatience-deep-cause-western-failure-handling-pandemic. I thank Jorge Aliaga for bringing this interesting article to my attention.

17 Sigmund Freud develops this idea in "Formulations on the Two Principles of Mental Functioning" (1911b) and in "Beyond the Pleasure Principle" (1920). For Donald Winnicott, see *The Family and the Outside World* (Baltimore: Penguin Books, 1964), *Home Is Where We Start From: Essays by a Psychoanalyst* (Harmondsworth: Penguin, 1986), and above all *The Maturational Processes and the Facilitating Environment* (London: Hogarth, 1965). Experiments in neuroscience have also ratified that the capacity to postpone gratification has its correlate in the effectiveness in the performance of different tasks.

18 This notion is fully compatible with the ideas of Zygmunt Bauman, Richard Sennett, or Ullrich Beck. See Zygmunt Bauman, *Postmodern Ethics* (Cambridge, MA: Basil Blackwell); *Liquid Modernity* (Cambridge: Polity, 2000); and *Community. Seeking Safety in an Insecure World* (Cambridge: Polity, 2001). See too Richard Sennett, *The Corrosion of Character: The Personal Consequences of Work in the New Capitalism* (London and New York: W. W. Norton & Company, 1998). See too Ulrich Beck, *Risk Society: Towards a New Modernity* (London and New York: Sage, 1992).

19 For more information on the changes and continuities in Latin American's social structure, one of the most up-to-date and thought-provoking works is that of Gabriela Benza and Gabriel Kessler, *La ¿nueva? estructura social de América Latina. Cambios y persistencias después de la ola de gobiernos progresistas* (Buenos Aires: Siglo XXI, 2020). I am especially grateful to Gabriel Kessler for sending me an advanced copy of this interesting work.

20 For an analysis of the role of criminal organizations in pandemics in Latin America, see this most interesting work by Steven Dudley and Jeremy McDermott, "Game Changers 2020. How Organized Crime Survived the

Pandemic," *InSight Crime*, December 21, 2020, https://insightcrime.org/news/analysis/gamechangers-organized-crime-pandemic/.

21 Tomas Pueyo, "Coronavirus: The Hammer and the Dance. What the Next 18 Months Can Look Like, if Leaders Buy Us Time," March 19, 2020. https://tomaspueyo.medium.com/coronavirus-the-hammer-and-the-dance-be9337092b56.

22 The precautionary principle is a way of representing our relationship with the community in which we live. When we decide to adopt a set of precautions in the face of an unknown virus (not only so that we do not become infected but fundamentally so that we do not infect others), we assume cooperation as a guideline for our behavior. We do something for someone else in the hope that someone else will do it for us, and we find reassurance and encouragement in observing the positive results of the protective measures. The precautionary principle has a tradition that dates back to the 1970s, but was defined and recognized as such at the beginning of the 21st century by entities such as the World Commission on the Ethics of Scientific Knowledge and Technology of the United Nations Educational, Scientific, and Cultural Organization (UNESCO) in 2005 and the Argentine National Committee on Ethics in Science and Technology.

23 On August 11, 2020, the proposal, which had already been circulating for more than a month, was publicly presented in the City of Buenos Aires by a group called *Initiative for the Protection of Human Rights COVID-19*, with the participation of representatives of human rights organizations, researchers, and numerous organizations such as trade unions and health workers. Despite the insistence from August 2020 to July 2021, the proposal never gained the government's interest except for a brief period in May 2021 which, despite being successful, lasted only 21 days. It was then suspended and gave way to a fairly general reopening of activities.

24 Małgorzata Gruchoła and Małgorzata Sławek-Czochra, "The Culture of Fear" of Inhabitants of EU Countries in Their Reaction to the COVID-19 Pandemic – A Study Based on the Reports of the Eurobarometer," *Safety Science* 135 (2021), https://www.sciencedirect.com/science/article/pii/S0925753520305361.

Bibliography

Armstrong, R.A., A.D. Kane, E. Kursumovic, F.C. Oglesby and T.M. Cook, "Mortality in Patients Admitted to Intensive Care with COVID-19: An Updated Systematic Review and Meta-Analysis of Observational Studies," *Anaesthesia* 76 (2021): 537–548, https://doi.org/10.1111/anae.15425.

Bachelard, Gaston, *The Formation of the Scientific Mind. A Contribution to the Psychoanalisis of Objective Knowledge* (Manchester: Clinamen, 2002 [1938]).

Bachelard, Gaston, *The New Scientific Spirit* (Boston: Beacon Press, 1985).

Baker, Michael, N. Wilson and T. Blakely, "Elimination Could Be the Optimal Response Strategy for Covid-19 and Other Emerging Pandemic Diseases", *BMJ* 371 (2020): 1–4.

Balsa, Javier, "Strategies against the COVID-19 Pandemic and the Crisis of Hegemony," *Notebooks: The Journal for Studies on Power* 1, no. 1 (2021): 96–119, https://doi.org/10.1163/26667185-01010006.

Baudrillard, Jean, *The Consumer Society* (Paris: Gallimard, 1970 [1998]).

Bauman, Zygmunt, *Postmodern Ethics* (Cambridge: Basil Blackwell, 1993).

Bauman, Zygmung, *Liquid Modernity* (Cambridge: Polity, 2000).

Bauman, Zygmunt, *Community. Seeking Safety in an Insecure World* (Cambridge: Polity, 2001).

Bauman, Zygmunt, *Work, Consumerism and the New Poor* (Berkshire and New York: Open University Press, 2005).

Beck, Ulrich, *Risk Society: Towards a New Modernity* (London and New York: Sage, 1992).

Benza, Gabriela and Gabriel Kessler, *La ¿nueva? estructura social de América Latina. Cambios y persistencias después de la ola de gobiernos progresistas* (Buenos Aires: Siglo XXI, 2020).

Berger, Peter and Luckmann, Thomas L., *The Social Construction of Reality. A Treatise in the Sociology of Knowledge* (New York: Doubleday, 1966).

Callaway, Ewen, "Had COVID? You'll Probably Make Antibodies for a Lifetime," *Nature*, 26 May 2021, https://www.nature.com/articles/d41586-021-01442-9.

Correia, Sergio, Stephan Luck, and Emil Verner, "Pandemics Depress the Economy, Public Health Interventions Do Not: Evidence from the 1918 Flu," June 5, 2020, https://ssrn.com/abstract=3561560 or http://dx.doi.org/10.2139/ssrn.3561560.

Dubet, François, *Le temps des passions tristes. Inégalités et populism* (Paris: Éditions du Seuil et La République des Idées, 2019).

Dudley, Steven and Jeremy McDermott, "Game Changers 2020. How Organized Crime Survived the Pandemic", *InSight Crime*, December 21, 2020, https://insightcrime.org/news/analysis/gamechangers-organized-crime-pandemic/.

Durkheim, Émile, *Suicide: A Study in Sociology* (London: Routledge & Kegan Paul, 1952).

Freud, Sigmund, "Formulations on the Two Principles of Mental Functioning" (1911), in *The Standard Edition of the Complete Psychological Works of Sigmund Freud* (London: The Hogarth Press and the Institute of Psycho-Analisis, 1958), Volume XII.

Freud, Sigmund, "Beyond the Pleasure Principle" (1920), in *The Standard Edition of the Complete Psychological Works of Sigmund Freud* (London: The Hogarth Press and the Institute of Psycho-Analisis, 1955), Volume XVIII.

García, Rolando, *Sistemas complejos. Conceptos, método y fundamentación epistemológica de la investigación interdisciplinaria* (Barcelona: Gedisa, 2006).

Gruchoła, Małgorzata and Malgorzata Sławek-Czochra, "The Culture of Fear" of Inhabitants of EU Countries in Their Reaction to the COVID-19 Pandemic – A Study Based on the Reports of the Eurobarometer," *Safety Science* 135 (2021), https://www.sciencedirect.com/science/article/pii/S0925753520305361.

Halbwachs, Maurice, *The Cadres Sociaux de la Mémoire* (Paris: Alcan, 1925).

Jayyusi, Lena, "The Reflexive Nexus: Photo-Practice and Natural History," *Continuum: The Australian Journal of Media & Cultural Studies* 6, no. 2 (1993): 25–52, https://doi.org/10.1080/10304319309359397.

Johansson, Michael A., Talia M. Quandelacy, Sarah Kada, Pragati Venkata Prasad, Molly Steele, John T. Brooks, Rachel B. Slayton, Matthew Biggerstaff and Jay C. Butler, "SARS-CoV-2 Transmission from People without COVID-19

Symptoms," *JAMA Network Open* 4, no. 1, https://jamanetwork.com/journals/jamanetworkopen/fullarticle/2774707.

Milanović, Branko, "Impatience: A Deep Cause of Western Failure in Handling the Pandemic?" *Global Policy Journal*, December 15, 2020, https://www.globalpolicyjournal.com/blog/15/12/2020/impatience-deep-cause-western-failure-handling-pandemic.

Nietzsche, Friedrich, *Der Wille zur Macht. Eine Auslegung alles Geschehens*, edited by Max Brahn (Lepizig: Alfred Kröner Verlag, 1917).

Oliu-Barton, Miquel, B. Pradelski, P. Aghion, P. Artus, I. Kickbusch, J. Lazarus, D. Sridhar and S. Vanderslott, "SARS-Cov-2 Elimination, not Mitigation, Creates Best Outcomes for Health, the Economy, and Civil Liberties," *The Lancet* (2021): 1–3, https://doi.org/10.1016/S0140-6736(21)00978-8.

Piaget, Jean, *The Grasp of Consciousness: Action and Concept in the Young Child* (London: Routledge and Kegan Paul, 1977).

Piaget, Jean, *The Equilibration of Cognitive Structures: The Central Problem of Intellectual Development* (Chicago: University of Chicago Press, 1985).

Piaget, Jean and García, Rolando, *Psychogenesis and the History of Science* (New York: Columbia University Press, 1989).

Pueyo, Tomas, "Coronavirus: The Hammer and the Dance. What the Next 18 Months Can Look Like, if Leaders Buy Us Time," March 19, 2020, https://tomaspueyo.medium.com/coronavirus-the-hammer-and-the-dance-be9337092b56.

Rosch, Eleanor and Barbara B. Lloyd (eds), *Cognition and Categorization* (Hillsdale: Lawrence Erlbaum, 1978).

Sennett, Richard, *The Corrosion of Character: The Personal Consequences of Work in the New Capitalism* (London and New York: W. W. Norton & Company, 1998).

Winnicott, Donald, *The Family and the Outside World* (Baltimore: Penguin Books, 1964).

Winnicott, Donald, *The Maturational Processes and the Facilitating Environment* (London: Hogarth, 1965).

Winnicott, Donald, *Home Is Where We Start From: Essays by a Psychoanalyst* (Harmondsworth: Penguin, 1986).

2 Denial and other demons

The role of psychological defense mechanisms in the COVID-19 crisis

The representation of reality takes place on three interrelated levels: the cognitive, the emotional, and the ethical-moral. Each of these is made up of psychological and social elements. These include emotions and perceptions of reality; transgenerational inheritances; the effect of childhood attachments on our relationships; economic circumstances; and the epistemological obstacles created by our historical worldview. However, it is important to understand that these levels arise from processes of abstraction and that in reality they are highly interconnected.

Representations of natural and manmade catastrophes are often resistant to change at both the individual and collective level. This resistance is due largely to psychological defense mechanisms in general and various forms of denial in particular. To understand this process, we need to unravel the complex web that connects social representations to what Freud called "the unconscious."

Defense mechanisms

Sigmund Freud, the father of psychoanalysis, is widely known for his method of treating mental disorders through a dialogue between patient and analyst. Among his many discoveries as a therapist, one of the most important was what he called defense mechanisms. As human beings we are not able to accept everything that happens to us, and our feelings in the face of a perceived danger often become unbearable. Defense mechanisms are unconscious psychological maneuvers that protect us from the anxiety produced by internal and social conflicts.

Freud claimed that the mind has a "protective shield" against potentially harmful excitations from the outside world. However, traumatic events such as sexual abuse, domestic violence, armed combat, torture and genocide, natural disasters, serious accidents, or terminal illnesses (among others) are capable of breaking through this shield. This causes, in Freud's words, "the

DOI: 10.4324/9781003267614-3

problem of mastering the amounts of stimulus which have broken in and of binding them, in the psychical sense, so that they can be disposed of."[1] In such cases, our representation of the trauma may confront us with situations we are unable to incorporate into our image of reality and of who we are.

It is interesting to note that what one person finds intolerable, another person may deal with more resiliently. Each of us has a different psychological makeup that continues to develop throughout our lives. Trauma is not caused by events themselves but by the way we process them at any given moment. How we will react to a life-threatening situation is unpredictable and varies greatly from one individual and one situation to another.

However, there are situations which most people find difficult to accommodate within their prior structures of knowledge and experience. As a result, they will suffer, and in some cases their suffering may become traumatic. This type of situation is often described as a catastrophe or crisis. The COVID-19 pandemic constitutes just such an event because of the number of deaths involved, the percentage of the population affected, and the profound impact on people's daily lives caused by both the disease itself and the various restrictions imposed by the authorities.

Freud claims that in situations like these we resort to various defense mechanisms to avoid facing a reality we cannot handle. The main defense mechanism – the one to which Freud devoted a large part of his work and for which he is most remembered – is repression. Repression is an unconscious process that automatically removes unwanted ideas, memories, feelings, or impulses from consciousness and pushes them into the unconscious. At the same time, what Freud calls "secondary repression" removes any conscious material that is reminiscent of the repressed material – especially material that might trigger feelings and emotions associated with the repressed material. Freud calls this secondary material the "offshoots" of the experience. It was his discovery of repression that led Freud to theorize a three-part psychic apparatus with a conscious, an unconscious, and a preconscious system.

Nevertheless, repression is unlikely to succeed as a defense mechanism against large-scale catastrophes or crises, precisely because so many people are involved. As mentioned earlier, each of us has a different psychological makeup. An event that affects large numbers of people could not be erased completely since some would try to avoid registering the experience, but many others would devote serious attention to it. So repression alone would not block social representations of such events.

During and after the Argentine genocide, many sectors of society would have liked to have looked the other way and wiped the slate clean. They were prevented from doing so by the survivors and the relatives of the disappeared who doggedly refused to be silenced. The Thursday marches of the Mothers of Plaza de Mayo – women wearing white headscarves and carrying pictures of their disappeared children – made selective amnesia and erasure socially impracticable. So did the survivor testimonies that began to circulate even before the dictatorship was over.

Like genocide, the COVID-19 pandemic is clearly an event with the potential to cause suffering on a large scale by bringing to light anxieties, fears, and desires, and by evoking previous traumatic experiences. It confronts us with difficult and disruptive changes in our behavior and our understanding of reality, both present and future. It also confronts us – more tangibly and directly than is normally tolerable – with the possibility that we or our loved ones may die. However, any discussion of the pandemic in terms of repression – at least repression of its social representations – is bound to fail. Repression may account for some individuals' reactions, but the omnipresence of the pandemic in the media and in everyday life inevitably gives rise to social representations. This does not mean, however, that social representations are not affected by other unconscious defense mechanisms that seek to *distort* reality rather than erase it.

Over the years, Freud detected a broad set of defense mechanisms, each of which may cast more light on our reactions to the pandemic. Freud's daughter, Anna Freud, discussed ten of these, and since then their number has grown. Among these mechanisms we find *dissociation* – disconnecting from our feelings and carrying on as if nothing was happening; and *projection* – attributing our own painful feelings or ideas to other people. For example, when we cannot accept our angry feelings, we may accuse others of hostility. This alienates us from our experience in ways that will be discussed in the next chapter. Then we have *introjection* – adopting the ideas or behavior of people who seem better able to cope than us; *regression* – falling back into a previous or infantile way of thinking; and *reaction formation* – manifesting the opposite of the repressed desire. For example, a repressed homosexual may become homophobic. Finally, there is *isolation* – separation of feelings from ideas and events; *displacement* – redirecting sexual or aggressive impulses to a more acceptable or less threatening target; and various forms of *rationalization* – substituting an unacceptable but real reason for doing something for an acceptable one. This distorts our experience in various ways.

These defense mechanisms – especially *rationalization, reaction formation*, and *dissociation* – are important for analyzing individual responses to the COVID-19 pandemic. However, there is a specific set of defenses centered on *denial* that are essential to this discussion. In particular, Freud uses the term "disavowal" (*Verleugnung*), often translated as "denial," to denote an insistence that something unpleasant is not true despite strong evidence to the contrary. It leads to forms of rationalization that are easily transformed into social imaginaries or ideological constructs and that operate not only on our thought processes but also on our ability to perceive reality itself.

The mechanism of denial

Unlike repression, denial (or disavowal) does not erase the idea or perception in question but only its meaning. As Freud says, "Negation is a way of taking cognizance of what is repressed (...) The outcome of this is a kind of intellectual acceptance of the repressed, while at the same time what is essential to the repression persists."[2] We admit the facts but deny their importance – a combination of denial and rationalization.

During the COVID-19 pandemic, we have seen some of the different forms denial can take. Some people cling to the idea of omnipotence. The phenomenon exists, but will not affect me: "it only infects older people"; "my immune structure will protect me"; "my rituals will keep me safe"; "I am a lucky person." Others deny the reality of the pandemic outright: "the pandemic does not exist, it is an invention"; "the consequences of the pandemic are not so serious"; "we are exaggerating, it is a strong flu"; "the virus has never been identified." Yet others manifest their denial through dissociation. Although they admit the existence of the pandemic and its risks, they cannot relate this knowledge to their behavior and continue to act as if it did not exist.

This latter form of denial is interesting because psychoanalysis identifies *disavowal* as a specific type of denial linked to forms of dissociation. Disavowal allows the phenomenon to be perceived but not the consequences it entails for the person's belief system. This coexistence of unresolved contradictory perceptions may give rise to a form of *splitting*. As Octave Mannoni puts it tellingly, "I know but even so ...," where the ellipsis implies that my behavior is unaffected by what I know.[3] I continue acting as if the traumatic situation did not exist.

The forms of denial described above – especially "disavowal" combined with rationalization – typically occur in situations such as the current pandemic. Therefore, any intervention strategy must learn to confront and transform them if it is to respond effectively to the crisis at the level of social practices. It is impossible to manage a pandemic without taking into account defense mechanisms and their possible impact on people's perceptions of reality. However, this problem has been ignored by governments in much of the world. On the contrary, the authorities themselves have often fallen into denial. Politicians and officials have announced restrictions that were either not enforced or were lifted after a few days; they have announced tragedies that did not occur; and in some cases they have themselves broken the rules with impunity. All this has reinforced denial in the population, as well as destroying faith in government.

However, as we shall see, denial not only protects us from psychological pain; the rationalizations to which it gives rise help build an ideological framework which shapes our representations of reality. This adds a further layer of complexity to the dispute over representations.

Sartre and bad faith

In *Being and Nothingness*, Jean Paul Sartre takes our understanding of denial a step further by suggesting that denial and disavowal (unlike repression) are conscious forms of self-deception that not only protect us from pain, but also legitimize selfish feelings and behaviors. Sartre defines this habit of self-deception with exquisite precision as "bad faith" – not to be confused with colloquial usages of the term.

In this sense, Sartre states:

> Bad faith is often assimilated to lying. We may indifferently say that someone is exhibiting bad faith, or that he is lying to himself. Here we are willing to allow that bad faith consists in lying to oneself—on condition that "lying to oneself" is immediately distinguished from lying *tout court*. We can agree that lying is a negative attitude. But this negation does not bear on consciousness itself; it aims only at something transcendent. Indeed, the essence of the lie implies that the liar is fully aware of the truth he is disguising. We do not lie about something we do not know about; we do not lie in broadcasting a mistake of which one is oneself a victim; we do not lie when we get something wrong. The ideal of the liar is, then, a cynic in his consciousness who affirms the truth in itself and negates it in his words, while negating this negation for himself.[4]

And he adds:

> Of course, for the person exercising bad faith, it is still a matter of covering up an unpleasant truth or of presenting some pleasant error as the truth. In appearance therefore, bad faith has the structure of a lie. But what changes everything is that in bad faith it is from myself that I am concealing the truth. Thus the duality of deceiver and deceived is not present here.[5]

Sartre himself distinguishes something particularly interesting and which has to do with the epistemological obstacles to our perception of reality already mentioned. This is how he analyzes the ways in which bad faith can choose its own evidence:

> In consequence, a particular type of evidence appears: non-persuasive evidence. Bad faith apprehends facts that are evident, but it is resigned in advance not to be fulfilled by such evidence, not to be persuaded and transformed into good faith. The person in bad faith becomes humble and modest: he is aware, he says, that faith is a decision and that after each intuition one is obliged to determine what is and to will it. Thus, in its basic project and from the moment it arises, bad faith determines the precise nature of its requirements: it becomes visible in its entirety in its resolution not to ask for too much, to consider itself satisfied when it is poorly persuaded, to force through, by means of a decision, its adherence to uncertain truths. [...] One puts oneself into bad faith as one goes to sleep, and being in bad faith is like dreaming. Once this mode of being is actualized, it is as difficult to leave it as to wake up: the fact is that bad faith—like being awake or dreaming—is a type of being in the world that tends to perpetuate itself of its own accord, even though its structure is metastable in kind.[6]

This "bad faith" or self-deception succeeds because it makes our reactions seem appropriate. It manages to bypass our conscience or moral sense and enhances the protection afforded by denial and disavowal. Problems arise when we ignore these processes or when we assume that in certain circumstances, such as the current pandemic, denial and "bad faith" are inevitable. This simply reinforces the current state of affairs instead of challenging the culture of self-deception and complacency in an attempt to change it.

Pacts of denial

The transformation of individual defense mechanisms into social representations is mediated by different processes. René Kaës, a professor of psychology at the University of Lyon in France, is a specialist in psychoanalytic group therapy who has researched shared intrapsychic contents between generations and among members of groups, consisting among other things of patterns of repetition and shared ways of perceiving reality. In the following passage, Kaës explains how disavowal replaces repression through an unconscious pact of denial.[7] In psychoanalytic parlance, the "narcissistic contract" is our unconscious need for others which forms the basis of socialization, while a "screen memory" is a distorted memory.

The pact of denial also fulfills a transubjective repressive function in constituting memory; its unspoken formula could be: do not remember what could endanger our bond, which is more precious than the memory of what happened, for what happened has already happened to all of us. In this way, the pact of denial sustains the narcissistic contract; it contributes to the formation of shared screen memories: of myths, screen memories of [whole] peoples. The pact of denial also participates in the repetition through which catastrophic experience and trauma are expressed. Couples, families, groups, institutions and societies have patterns of repetition, each in their own way. They administer, therefore, the psychic repetitions that are underpinned therein and preserve them.[8]

Repetition compulsion in psychoanalytic theory is an unconscious need to repeat earlier experiences or actions. The pact of denial perpetuates this sort of repetition but at the same time establishes a consensus not to think about the repressed emotional aspects of the experiences or actions and to silence those who attempt to do so. Therefore, the negative pact is no longer something that functions in the mind of each individual but is rather a matter of behaviors linked to intersubjectivity, in other words, what occurs *between* people. The pact of denial does not operate only or fundamentally at the individual level but also at the social level.

As with denial or "bad faith" at the individual level, a pact of denial does not render a group unaware of what has happened or is happening. Neither does it blind them to the consequences or likely consequences. The group simply behaves as if the reality did not exist, hence the idea of a "pact" (the term is well chosen) that is never made explicit. It is never made explicit because, if it were, that in itself would be an acknowledgment of what we wish to ignore. For example, a family in which there is sexual abuse would fall apart as a family – the social bond could not be preserved – if the abuse were acknowledged openly. Therefore, although most of the family knows deep down what is really going on, nobody speaks about it. The victim may forget, sometimes for years or even decades, that they have been abused.

Pacts of denial are found in abusive families but also in wider social groups that try to ignore a collective catastrophe (for example, genocide). They continue with their lives as if nothing had happened, systematically avoiding any reference to the traumatic event. This does not mean, however, that there is no record of the event in the memory of those who subscribe to the "pact." In Spain and Chile, for example, countless families and, indeed, entire sectors of society and their political representatives behave as if the horrors perpetrated by Franco and Pinochet had never occurred. Even after more than 80 years in the case of Spain and 50 in the case of Chile, many refuse to deal with the consequences of what happened under the clichéd pretext of "looking forward, not backwards."

Such willful ignorance comes at a price. Filtered through this pact of denial, trauma undermines people's belief in themselves and their feelings. In societies that have undergone catastrophes such as genocide, it destroys any remaining self-confidence and prevents the survivors from owning their history. It transforms them into strangers to their own experience, alienating them from historical accounts of what happened and the possibility of relating these to their own experience. In Spain, for example, survivors of what Paul Preston calls the "Spanish Holocaust" repeatedly mention the enormous difficulties they face in making their voices heard.[9] This was also found among the survivors of Nazism (at least until the 1980s) and the Argentine genocide.[10] Even today, survivor testimonies continue to be minimized or denied in comparison with the testimonies of relatives of the disappeared.

Pacts of denial produce patterns of collective alienation and distancing. Narratives are structured as stories that happened to *others*, and they deliberately exclude the first person. Despite what studies of disavowal, bad faith, and self-deception might suggest, however, this is not a conscious conspiracy. Rather, narratives emerge and become accepted because they are consistent with people's psychological needs, defense mechanisms, and search for identity. This is the reason for their success.

Returning now to the COVID-19 pandemic, the concept of pacts of denial may help account for some of the social consequences of the catastrophe. For the most part, the media have focused attention away from the dead and their relatives, testimonies from health personnel have been scarce, and an anonymous register of the "numbers" of dead and infected has artificially restricted broader discussion of the consequences of the disease. The Spanish novelist and journalist, Arturo Pérez-Reverte, has drawn attention to this fact in an article entitled "We did not see enough bodies," while Argentine sociologist, Malena Silveyra, compares this with the absence of the disappeared in the Argentine genocide.[11,12] However, despite these warnings, the dead and the sick have remained almost invisible.

This does not mean that the pandemic has not been discussed endlessly. On the contrary, it was the main topic of media attention in most countries of the world during 2020. However, references to death have gradually been silenced by pacts of denial that filter out the most painful aspects of the pandemic. It is common to see guests on talk shows insult those who try to bring up sensitive issues although it is true that this has not happened everywhere in the same way. In contrast, the impact of school closures and online learning, the anguish of social isolation during the global pandemic, and the economic consequences of lockdown have received much greater media coverage. Putting a face to the victims or to the overworked health personnel who struggle to save them does not merit high enough ratings. Therefore, these pictures of the pandemic have not gone viral except for a few cases in the early weeks, when cemeteries in places like Guayaquil or New York could not cope with the number of burials. But even then, death was depersonalized and anonymized. Pictures of mass graves lasted just a few weeks before the media moved on to more congenial topics – and before anyone could come to terms with the traumatic consequences of all this.

Finally, a traumatic event such as the COVID-19 pandemic may not only *desensitize* individuals but also contribute to the social and historical accumulation of trauma within a society. One way of coping when our "protective shield" is overwhelmed is to turn the numbness this causes into a more general desensitization by mentally disconnecting from other environmental stimuli. This is an adaptive response to pain when the latter cannot be avoided or confronted.

When it relates to events affecting large population groups, this *accumulated desensitization* makes it difficult to identify with the victims of the denied experience, especially once they have been depersonalized. During the COVID-19 pandemic, we have noticed a growing indifference in society to the victims and their relatives, as well as to health workers, whose suffering has only increased by the day.

This indifference is seen in the debate that began in Latin America at the end of 2020 and the beginning of 2021 about who had suffered most during the pandemic. Following attempts to scapegoat young people in the summer of 2020, there was an attempt to construct children as the main victims because of the loss of face-to-face schooling. However, the dead themselves and the health workers who cared for the seriously ill were increasingly absent from this debate. It was as if not mentioning death had magically made it disappear.

The general lack of tributes, remembrance services, and other opportunities to mourn the victims of COVID-19 has become common in much of the Western world. Families have not had the opportunity to grieve in a timely manner. In many cases, they have not even been able to say goodbye to their loved ones. In Argentina this topic has been the subject of several important in-depth sociological studies, such as that conducted by Veronica Giordano.[13] Not surprisingly, these studies have received much less attention in the media than other research. Media prominence would mean a radical break with the pacts of denial that seek to exclude death and the personalization of the dead from public debate.

Denialism as an ideological construct and rationalization

At the level of social relations, denial can be translated into different kinds of rationalization organized by ideological frameworks. Indeed, one of the most common forms of representation throughout history in response to catastrophic realities has been denialism. This ideological and political construct exploits the psychic phenomena of denial, disavowal, naturalization, self-deception, and various denial pacts. Now, this may seem harmless on the face of it. After all, mental defense systems seek to protect us from experiences we cannot assimilate into a broader narrative at a particular moment in our lives. However, when it comes to collective representations that guide social action, the combined working of these defense systems with rationalizations can have devastating effects.

Denialism is a common response to catastrophes such as wars, genocides, earthquakes, or tsunamis. It needs to be disarmed if a society wishes to respond to these events effectively. In other words, society must transform the responses it had before the disruptive phenomenon appeared. Fortunately, it is relatively easy to confront social representations as long as we remember that they are dynamic and unstable and that their cognitive, emotional, and moral components are interrelated.

During the Nazi era, European Jews often developed strategies of denial. For example, they downplayed or refused to believe explicit threats by Nazi leaders; they rejected or ignored the testimonies of survivors who had escaped from concentration camps; and when deportation from the ghettos to the death camps became imminent, they hoped that their labor might mean life. Their belief in the face of all evidence that the Nazis would put rational economic goals and winning the war before the irrational aims of extermination was just one example of denial, self-deception, and pacts.

It is enlightening to read the testimonies of leaders of the Jewish resistance groups and the way they identified these issues as a major political problem. Marek Edelman, leader of the Jewish Bund workers' party in the Warsaw ghetto, recounts that as the mass shooting of tens of thousands of Jews reached the ghetto in November 1941, "The majority was still of the opinion that the murders were not a result of an organized, orderly policy to exterminate the Jewish people, but acts of misbehavior on the part of victory-drunk troops."[14] Edelman notes that when over 50 people were dragged from their homes by German soldiers and shot in the ghetto streets one night in April 1942,

The majority [of the Jewish population of the ghetto] came to the conclusion that the action was aimed at editors of clandestine papers, and that all illegal activities should have been stopped so as not to need-lessly increase the tremendous number of victims.[15]

Nazi propaganda itself also took its effect, by encouraging various forms of denial and self-deception. Edelman describes this in a heartbreaking way:

> In the meantime the Germans, not too discriminating in their choice of methods, introduced a new propaganda twist. They promised – and actually gave – three kilograms of bread and one kilogram of mar-malade to everyone who voluntarily registered for "deportation." The offer was more than sufficient. Once the bait was thrown, propaganda and hunger did the rest. The propaganda value of the measure lay in the fact that it was truly an excellent argument against the "stories" about gas chambers ("why would they be giving bread away if they intended to murder them?"). The hunger, an even stronger persuader, magnified the picture of three brown, crusty loaves of bread until nothing was vis-ible beyond it. Their taste which one could almost feel in one's mouth – it was only a short walk from one's home to the "Umschlagplatz" from which the cars left – blinded people to all the other things at the end of the same road. Their smell, familiar, delicious, befogged one's mind, made it unable to grasp the things which would normally have been so very obvious. There were times when hundreds of people had to wait on line for several days to be "deported." The number of people anx-ious to obtain the three kilograms of bread was such that the transports, now leaving twice daily with 12,000 people, could not accommodate them all.[16]

Despite the obvious differences between the Nazi genocide and the COVID-19 pandemic, parallels can be drawn between the different forms of self-justification, self-denial, or denial that thrived during both catastrophes. Many of the discourses arising from the COVID-19 pandemic, especially "a return to everyday life" (parties, meetings, outings, etc.) have acted as familiar and delicious smells to befog our minds. They have hidden the reality of saturated emergency rooms and intensive care units, sick and dead relatives, and the relentless spread of the virus and its variants, which has turned public spaces into danger areas. It is also interesting to note how negative emotions have been transferred from the pandemic itself onto the restrictions designed to control it. Anger with public policy decisions is a way of denying the threat of death to our loved ones or the population as a whole.

Jewish resistance groups in Nazi-occupied territories identified the prob-lem early on, and they did so very precisely. They recognized that one of their main political tasks was to confront denial openly and explicitly. Moreover, they realized that armed resistance was pointless unless the majority of the population faced up to what was happening and stopped trying to rationalize or deny it. The failure of the uprisings in Bialystok and Vilnius in August and September 1943 was attributed to the impossibility of breaking denial in the majority of the population. On the other hand, overcoming denial was crucial in obtaining a high level of support for the Warsaw ghetto uprising. Lasting from April 19 to May 16, 1943, this became the best known act of Jewish resistance to Nazism because it involved almost the entire surviving ghetto population, unlike what happened in most other towns or cities where denial was rampant.[17]

Something similar happened during the last Argentine dictatorship, when society tried to convince itself that the military could not have murdered so many people. Rumors circulated that detainees were being sent to "recovery farms" in the south of the country and that the disappeared were hiding in Europe. During the first two years of the Argentine genocide, these lies were believed even by some of the relatives of the disappeared. Denouncing the dictatorship's human rights violations was branded as part of a campaign instigated by foreign powers and exiled members of insurgent organizations to tarnish the country's reputation. Indeed, during the visit in 1979 of the Inter-American Commission on Human Rights, most of population supported an official campaign with posters and stickers that punned: "Argentineans are human and right." This was just one of many forms of self-deception that were practiced at the time to avoid coming to terms with the disappearance and death of thousands of fellow citizens.

As we have just seen, individuals and societies react to catastrophes in ways that are well understood by psychologists, sociologists, and historians. It is surprising, then, that little attention was paid at the beginning of the COVID-19 pandemic – and later – to the risk that health care strategies would be undermined by denial. Politicians and health officials barely discussed the problem, nor did sociologists or even psychologists. Argentina has a long tradition of professional associations participating in public life. However, the first statements by the Argentine College of Psychoanalysts did not appear until July and August 2020. And they were mostly ignored by the rest of society.

Denial as an ideological framework

As we have seen, denial is a defense mechanism that can take different forms. Bad faith – playing it safe and acting as if we are not free to choose – is a form of self-deception with a moral and ethical dimension, and it is often linked to denial. Disavowal, dissociation, and avoidance are all ways of detaching ourselves individually from a traumatic experience, while pacts of denial allow us to avoid processing the traumatic experience at the social level.

At the same time, denial at the individual level can give rise to an ideological framework and social representations of reality based on rationalizations.

Stanley Cohen has analyzed this phenomenon most perceptively with respect to different social processes in his classic book *States of Denial: An Essay on Atrocities and Suffering*, which shows how denial can take many faces. Here we will explore just four of these. I have chosen them because of their historical importance and because they can be seen in relation to the COVID-19 pandemic: (a) relativism or minimization; (b) false analogy; (c) oversimplification; and (d) conspiracy theories.

Relativism or minimization

Relativism or minimization is a classic form of rationalization that is no longer individual but collective. It is found in expressions such as "there are not so many dead," and reports that repeatedly underestimate the number of deaths in the total population. It is also found in the insistence that the coronavirus only poses a serious threat to the elderly and to patients with comorbidities, as if this justified the rest of society abandoning them to their fate. In short, it constructs the news about the catastrophe as exaggerated and alarmist.

A similar notion can be found in the perceptions of German and Polish Jews that the murders, tortures, and kidnappings perpetrated by the Nazis only affected political militants. In fact, this was true in Germany from 1933 to 1938 and in Warsaw during the first years of the Second World War II, just as it is true that the pandemic has mostly killed elderly people and those with pre-existing medical conditions.

Just world thinking is the assumption of a stable, controllable, beneficent world.[18] Cohen points out that people who believe in a just world are more likely to believe that victims deserve their fate. Many Jews thought they would be safe if they avoided "dangerous" activities and distanced themselves from those who were being murdered. They argued that the bulk of the population was not involved in politics and, therefore, would not be affected. *Just world thinking* and the reallocation of responsibility are also to be found in the COVID-19 pandemic. In the case of the pandemic, however, there is no way to stop being elderly or having a previous illness. *Just world thinking*, then, not only justifies and normalizes the death of part of the population, it accepts COVID-driven euthanasia of the old and infirm as the price for not disturbing the social life of the younger population for a few weeks or months. This attitude is all too visible in complaints about the suffering of adolescents during lockdown and the negative consequences of online schooling. In the case of education, these complaints have been accompanied by urgent demands for a return of face-to-face classes at whatever cost – even for teachers.

Unfortunately, however, this minimization of reality has not been limited to just world thinking. It has also included outright lies – e.g. that the mortality rate for COVID-19 and influenza are similar – and a reluctance to consider the long-term development of the pandemic. Consequently, during periods in which relatively few people were dying, little attention was paid to growth curves and projections forecasting a massive circulation of the virus in the near future. Similarly, few thought about the short- or long-term sequelae of infection for survivors of any age. In this way, one of the fundamental elements of the social bond was broken and an "every man for himself" approach emerged. Although this approach could be reversed at any time, each economic sector, social class, or generational group currently seems to observe the crisis only from the point of view of its particular interests. There has been no attempt to achieve a balanced view. Thus, perfectly correct information about the negative consequences of online schooling and the lack of social contact among young people are used as excuses to dismantle health care measures without knowing whether this will do more harm than good. Yet ultimately, the right to life must take precedence over other rights, no matter how painful it may be to place restrictions on the latter.

This type of relativism and minimization enshrines another danger. If we decide to abandon the elderly to their fate during the COVID-19 pandemic, we are much more likely to do the same with other population groups at moments of social crisis. I am thinking particularly of the poor and the unemployed; of victims of natural disasters such as droughts, fires, and floods, and refugees from civil wars; of women victims of violence; and of infants threatened with childhood diseases. Just as the COVID-19 crisis has created a victim group based on age and health, a different catastrophe, such as a war, an economic crisis, or a natural disaster could create different categories of victim based on age, gender, social class, or inclusion in the labor market.

Legitimizing the notion that specific population groups do not deserve our collective response dissolves the social bond on which communities have traditionally relied. Accepting that "old people were going to die *anyway*" is no different from saying that "the poor are going to live fewer years or in conditions of overcrowding or malnutrition *anyway*," that "refugees have little chance of survival *anyway*," or that "youngsters living in poor neighborhoods are going to fall victim to police violence *anyway*." Let us be absolutely clear about the importance of the social bond for survival. Left to their own devices and abilities, most of humanity would probably not be able to subsist, particularly in the complex economies of the 21st century with their highly specialized division of labor. The increasingly uncritical acceptance of an individualistic and profoundly selfish morality is one of the most terrible lessons of this pandemic.

Unfortunately, in the case of the COVID-19 pandemic, there are also specific factors that encourage minimization and relativism. Firstly, the deaths are difficult to count. With health systems collapsing in a matter of days and poor data management in many countries, it has been difficult to separate deaths *from* coronavirus from those *with* coronavirus or those from other causes. Much of Latin America, for example, has had to wait a year and a half for reliable information. Only now, as death rates are compared with those of previous years, are we gradually beginning to obtain a more accurate picture. This type of analysis shows significant underreporting of deaths due to COVID-19 in many countries of the world in the order of between 10 and 50 percent. These figures take into account a decrease in some causes of deaths, such as traffic accidents or other transmissible diseases, as a result of lockdowns.

As we have just seen, comparing mortality rates country by country with respect to pre-COVID-19 averages takes time. It is likely, then, that many denialist narratives will remain widespread for some time to come for lack of "confirmation" of the lethal impact of the pandemic. Indeed, this confirmation may come too late. Several erroneous notions about the pandemic became salient in social representations almost from the outset. These include the totally unfounded idea that all hospital deaths were being reported as COVID-19 related, something that is totally disproved by measurements of the excess death rate during the pandemic.

Another factor that encourages strategies of minimization and relativism is the time between infection and death, which is around 20 days. Thus, the daily death toll always underestimates the true seriousness of the situation when the contagion rate is growing. This is compounded by a so-called exponential growth bias that distorts social perceptions of the pandemic. Exponential growth bias is the universal tendency of people to perceive a growth process as linear even when it is in fact exponential. Thus, most people will see a two-fold increase in infections from 10,000 to 20,000 over a period of 25 days as being much more serious than a 20-fold increase in infections from 100 to 2,000 over the same time period. However, the reality is that over the next 50 days, those 2,000 cases will become 800,000 ($2,000 \times 20 \times 20$) whereas the 20,000 cases will become 80,000 ($20,000 \times 2 \times 2$). Research shows that people who misunderstand the math about how coronavirus spreads are less concerned about

COVID-19 and less likely to engage in social distancing, hand washing, or mask wearing.[19]

The combination of exponential growth bias and the "delay effect" (the time between contagion and death) may mean that attempts to produce a turnaround come too late. Many Western countries such as United States, United Kingdom, Italy, and Spain, among others, have reacted and continue to react late. Their relationship with time – in particular, the tendency to "live the moment" mentioned in the previous chapter – prevents them from understanding the importance of the precautionary principle, the "delay effect," and the exponential growth. Most of these countries identified the seriousness of the situation too late and, paradoxically, lifted restrictions too early, as soon as a slight improvement was observed. Impatience led to confusing improvement with the end of the cycle, which was obviously wrong.

As a result of these factors, the COVID-19 restrictions in most of these countries have proved ineffective. Many Western societies have suffered the economic and social consequences of lockdown with very few health benefits, since they could not wait long enough to flatten the contagion curve. This applies as much to government decisions as to social behavior. Proper health measures are not taken until hospitals are collapsing. At the first sign of improvement, precautions are abandoned before their effects have even begun to be felt. The inability to postpone gratification transforms many contemporary Western societies into a host of anxious children incapable of any medium- or long-term action. These societies and their leaders are drowning in data – voting results, opinion polls, health figures, even popularity ratings – but they are unable to plan for more than a few weeks ahead. In short, they are incapable of organizing a strategy to fight the pandemic.

Interestingly, minimization and relativism have not been exclusive to *explicitly* denialist governments, such as Trump's in the United States or Bolsonaro's in Brazil. They have also permeated political action elsewhere. Argentina's government under President Alberto Fernandez, for example, recognized the seriousness of the pandemic early in 2020 and took steps to strengthen the health system and prevent the virus from circulating. However, a general lack of understanding about how denial works not only led to irresponsible behavior among the population but to attitudes of avoidance and denial by the authorities themselves. This was seen in numerous public appearances by President Alberto Fernandez, who repeatedly insisted on the importance of respecting preventive health measures but did not apply them either in his private life or in his televised public addresses. Indeed, he seemed to grow tired of the "lack of results" and abandoned attempts to control the situation after August and September 2020.

What is striking is that this U-turn occurred precisely when the situation was critical in most of the country but was improving in the large urban area of Greater Buenos Aires. This confirmed the central role of the city of Buenos Aires in the construction of social representations in Argentina even though the country is a federal state with 24 provinces. Most of the president's television appearances dealt with the situation in Greater Buenos Aires, ignoring the rest of the country. Publicly, he neither praised the success of Argentina's provinces in containing the virus between April and July 2020 nor regretted the severity of the pandemic in the same provinces between August and November 2020.

False analogy

The second important form of denial is *false analogy*. We can find it in comparisons between deaths from COVID-19 and deaths related to road accidents or respiratory diseases. The reasoning behind these analogies is: why should we change our daily routine now if we have not done so to prevent these other causes of death? The answer is simple. Leaving aside the problem of underreporting, deaths from COVID-19 have clearly surpassed those from road accidents and from serious respiratory diseases such as influenza in every country where the virus has been allowed to circulate. And it was obvious from the beginning of the pandemic that this would happen: it was simply a matter of time.

But the analogy itself is false. Admittedly, many people die each year from respiratory diseases. These are the second or third leading cause of death among the elderly in most Western countries. But people do not die as a result of an unknown virus for which there is no vaccine or treatment and whose long-term effects are still unknown. All deaths are regrettable, but the incidence, causes, treatment, and sequelae of most medical conditions and accidents are well understood. Of course, strategies could be put in place to reduce deaths from the causes already mentioned, e.g. road safety campaigns, harsher penalties for dangerous drivers, more effective vaccination programs, or better hospitals. But we are dealing with knowable entities. The precautionary principle applies precisely in a new situation, when the forecast is uncertain and the severity undetermined.

To put it another way, when faced with an unknown virus, any analogy is false because it compares known figures against unknown, dynamic, and changing ones. It is true that the number of deaths from COVID-19 might not have been much higher than deaths from other known problems and that insistence on the precautionary principle might, in some cases and with hindsight, seem exaggerated. But the whole point of the precautionary principle is to take preventive action in the face of uncertainty. The precautionary principle is a concept best summed up by the proverb "better safe than sorry." Thus, preventive action is continued only until the situation becomes known and controllable by other means.

The application of the precautionary principle during the COVID-19 pandemic has not been exaggerated. Deaths from COVID-19 both in absolute and relative numbers have so far exceeded those from any previous pandemic since the so-called Spanish flu at the beginning of the 20th century. In the case of COVID-19, however, the extent to which the virus will continue to spread and mutate is unknown. There are no precedents and no definitive numbers. No country's population has reached herd immunity. As of September 2021, for example, only slightly more than half of the US population had been fully vaccinated against COVID-19 and young children were still not eligible for the vaccine.[20]

No one knows what will happen in the long-term. But it seems unlikely that the incidence of COVID-19 will even be reduced to the level of measles – at least not in the US.[21] As in the case of influenza, vaccines will likely have to be updated each year as the virus mutates to survive the immunity already present in the population. Therefore, until the pandemic is over, we cannot know whether the worst still lies ahead. New variants of the virus may cause second infections more severe than the first, or target different age groups, or produce irreversible sequelae in the neurological, cardiac, or respiratory systems in those who recover. This is the central argument for applying the precautionary principle. A worst case scenario cannot be ruled out in advance with the available data.

False analogies undermine the precautionary principle. They assume without any objective evidence that the current pandemic will develop in ways similar to previous pandemics. This is a mere gamble that could cause a massive death toll and even the extinction of the human race if we were unlucky enough to get it wrong. It is clear that betting on minimization or false analogies instead of implementing the precautionary principle does not make sense as a survival strategy, much less as a guide for social action.

Oversimplification

The third important form of denial is *oversimplification*: looking for quick and easy answers to deal with something complex and unknown. There are plenty of examples of oversimplification that are closely related to relativism/minimization and false analogy. One was the insistence for several months that the solution to the pandemic lay in "more testing." Now, testing is necessary for statistical purposes, but the test–trace–isolate approach works only in neighborhoods where people have relatively large homes and can work remotely. For those living in overcrowded tenements and shanty towns, isolation is almost impossible.

A further example of oversimplification was the number of urban myths that began to circulate. In Argentina the media began to complain about "the longest quarantine in the world" (reflecting the classic

Argentine desire to be unique and special). Groups such as hairdressers, joggers, and young people were blamed for spreading the virus. Attempts were made to import models from South Korea, Germany, Sweden, and Uruguay, countries with very different social, economic, and health systems, as if they were magic remedies that could be applied everywhere. Unfortunately, these models failed or proved problematic even in their countries of origin.

Many Argentinians see themselves as COVID-19 epidemiologists, just as they see themselves as coaches for the national soccer team. Like supporters shouting advice to players from the stands, they demand a change of tactics from the authorities every week. They do not understand why these measures are not being implemented when bad reporting by non-specialist media explains so clearly how easy the solutions are. At the same time, many of these would-be epidemiologists ignore existing public health regulations, regardless of whether these are more or less effective or appropriate. Paradoxically, the two faces of individualism contradict each other.

During the pandemic we have seen a large number of people making their own rules. These personal rules, based on Google searches and opinions in social networks, have in turn made individual behavior unpredictable. In this way, oversimplification has created profound obstacles to implementing concerted social actions to cope with the pandemic and has generated a situation of growing anomie in many Western countries.

Social representations of the pandemic, then, are no longer based on objective science as would have been the case a few decades ago. Instead, scientific objectivity is being replaced by an increasingly harmful relativism (both epistemological and moral).

Now, it is one thing to describe a phenomenon and a very different thing to accept and legitimize it. A catastrophe cannot be tackled merely by uncoordinated, individual actions. It is totally unacceptable that public health measures should be "negotiated" or applied according to personal criteria, just as it would be unacceptable to leave aviation safety to the whims of individual pilots and air traffic controllers.[22]

Among other things, a society is a group of individuals that works together to pursue common goals, the most basic of which is the survival of its members. Thus, cooperation lies at the heart of society. Through its leaders and representatives, society has a *right* to demand that individuals cooperate in fighting a pandemic that puts everyone at risk. The alternative – the abandoning of concerted action – leads to a breakdown of values and a sense of futility and lack of purpose that are unlikely to solve anything.

Numerous social scientists, including Max Weber, Antonio Gramsci, and Norbert Elias, have pointed out that norms are imposed either by coercion or by consensus. Although the latter is generally preferable, sometimes there is neither the time nor the opportunity for consensus building, and a degree of coercion is required to protect the population as a whole. Crises such as wars or natural disasters are prime examples. A population cannot be consulted when faced with the need to evacuate a city because of a tsunami, a flood, or an earthquake, nor is there time to argue with those who consider the risks to be debatable. Restrictions on the spread of an unknown virus cannot be decided by plebiscite, any more than the state's response to the bombing of a city or the tactics chosen to defend a strategic sector during a war. Norms in such contexts cannot be "negotiable" or "optional."

Conspiracy theories

The fourth and final form of denial is *conspiracy theories.* These simultaneously appeal to the fascist right, to another right calling itself "libertarian," and to a denunciationist cultural left, a pathetic example of which has been Italian academic Giorgio Agamben's denunciations of a generalized "state of exception" and his idea of an "invented pandemic."[23] More generally, conspiracy theories reflect all sorts of left-wing and right-wing "anti-politics" in the broad sense of the term.

In the context of the pandemic, the linchpin of all conspiracy theories is the idea that the coronavirus is a hoax perpetrated to secretly control or manipulate us. These theories incorporate many existing ingredients: the big business of Big Pharma; the bureaucracy of international organizations like the World Health Organization; anger against "politics" and corrupt politicians; modern state disciplining based on electronic surveillance and control; and 21st century state-of-exception provisions to deal with emergencies. Hence, conspiracy theories appeal to many people who feel that their freedoms are threatened – in some cases, they appeal to whole sectors of society.

This does not mean that administrations have not taken advantage of the pandemic to clamp down on the population and strengthen government power. Police repression in Colombia, for example, has been particularly brutal, but many countries have adopted measures during the COVID-19 pandemic that are either disproportionate or illegal. Nevertheless, that is quite different from equating compulsory health care measures *themselves* with repression. Unfortunately, academics and politicians who should know better have been remarkably irresponsible in their public statements. In Argentina, for example, 300 scientists, intellectuals, and journalists published a letter in May 2020 complaining about an "infectatorship." They accused the government of using the pandemic to dismantle the separation of powers between executive, legislative, and judiciary.

Obviously, it is absurd to liken public health measures to the decrees of a dictator or to equate the "care-neglect" continuum with the "authoritarianism-freedom" one. Freedom does not exist in a vacuum. Freedom is comparative and is always subject to conditions and restrictions. It is not possible to enjoy any freedom when one's own life is at stake. Thus, every community must give up certain freedoms for the survival of the whole.

The balance between individual freedom and collective rights was preached by the founders of liberal thought (Rousseau, Locke, and Montesquieu) and by those who advocated rebellion against the established order (Marx, Lenin, and Mao Zedong). It was also theorized by several fathers of modern sociology (Émile Durkheim, Max Weber, Norbert Elias, and Pierre Bourdieu). The questions here are (among others): what freedoms should be suspended during the COVID-19 pandemic and for how long? How are they related to the dangers of the pandemic? What is the overall strategy for coping with the pandemic into which the suspension of freedoms must fit? What are the consequences of suspending these freedoms and how can we demonstrate that they are less serious than the damage the pandemic itself could cause? These are just some of the questions that require precise, accurate, and informed answers and cannot be approached in a simplistic manner.

Effects of defense mechanisms and ideological frameworks on social action

A pandemic confronts us with two problems linked to denial mechanisms. Firstly, countless people – including many who fully understand the seriousness of the situation – have developed dysfunctional emotional reactions that hinder or prevent public health care measures. These individuals understand the problem but are unable to micro-manage the dozens of daily encounters they could avoid or handle differently. A good example is television studios, which have generally failed to implement minimum safeguards against the virus. Not only are the studios themselves important centers of contagion, there is a double discourse in the explicit messages of TV guests and presenters, on the one hand, and their non-verbal communication, on the other. But we can also find this type of denial in the widespread misuse of face masks (hanging below the nose), family gatherings in closed spaces, and friends who do not follow social distancing norms. Here, and in many other cases, disavowal and other denial mechanisms are clearly at work.

Secondly, we have population groups whose actions cannot be explained by lack of awareness or carelessness alone. These people have been directly affected by *rationalized* denial. They appeal to minimizing strategies, conspiracy theories, oversimplification, or false analogies to consciously defend and give a meaning to their actions. Consequently, politicians, civil servants, media specialists, and designers of information campaigns as well as professional bodies and health personnel need to understand how denial works in order to deal with the pandemic effectively. In this sense, the fight is also a political one in that changing people's social behavior depends on winning the battle for common sense.

Notes

1 Sigmund Freud, "Beyond the Pleasure Principle" (1920). *The Standard Edition of the Complete Works of Sigmund Freud* 18, edited and translated by James Strachey (London: Hogarth Press, 1968), 30.
2 Sigmund Freud, "Negation," in *On Metapsychology*, The Pelican Freud Library, vol. 11 (Harmondsworth: Penguin Books, 1977), 437.
3 Octave Mannoni, *La otra escena. Claves de lo imaginario* (Buenos Aires: Amorrortu, 1979).
4 Jean-Paul Sartre, *Being and Nothingness: An Essay in Phenomenological Ontology*, translated by Sarah Richmond (First Washington Square Press/Atria Paperback, 2021), 153.
5 Ibid., 154.
6 Ibid., 178.
7 Other terms for "pact of denial" are "negation pact" and "denegative pact."
8 Janine Puget and René Kaës (comp.), *Violencia de Estado y psicoanálisis* (Buenos Aires y México: Lumen, 2006), 177.
9 See: Paul Preston, *The Spanish Holocaust: Inquisition and Extermination in Twentieth-Century Spain* (London: Harper Collins, 2012).
10 Daniel Feierstein, *Genocide as Social Practice. Reorganizing Society under Nazism and the Argentina Military Juntas* (New Jersey: Rutgers University Press, 2014).
11 Arturo Pérez-Reverte, "No vimos bastantes muertos" [We Didn't See Enough Bodies], *XLSemanal*, https://www.xlsemanal.com/firmas/20200822/no-vimos -bastantes-muertos-perez-reverte.html.
12 Malena Silveyra, "A mí no me van a pasar" [It Won't Happen to Me], *Tiempo Argentino,* September 2, 2020, https://www.tiempoar.com.ar/nota/a-mi-no-me -va-a-pasar.
13 The Network of Care, Rights, and Decisions at the End of Life of the National Council for Scientific and Technical Research (CONICET) and, in particular, Verónica Giordano, played a key role in analyzing different forms of grief. Among the numerous materials produced, the report entitled "Death and Grief in the Context of the COVID-19 Pandemic," which was signed by all the members of the Network in August 2020, is particularly noteworthy. Available at: https:// redcuidados.conicet.gov.ar/wp-content/uploads/sites/148/2020/10/El-duelo-en -contexto-de-pandemia-septiembre-2020.pdf.
14 Marek Edelman, *The Ghetto Fights,* first published in Polish in Warsaw, 1945 (London: The Russell Press, 2013), 29–30.
15 Ibid., 35–36.

16 Ibid., 42.
17 For a critical analysis of the various Jewish rebellions in the ghettos established by the Nazis and the role of denial as the main difficulty, the testimony of Haika Grossman is brilliant. As a courier between the various ghettos, Grossman had a first-hand perception of the different situations. See Haika Grossman, *The Underground Army: Fighters of the Bialystok Ghetto* (Holocaust Library, 1988). Also, for a comparative analysis of many of these elements and dozens of testimonies, see Daniel Feierstein, *Nuevos estudios sobre genocidio* (Mexico: Heredad, 2020).
18 Stanley Cohen, *States of Denial: Knowing about Atrocities and Suffering* (Cambridge, UK: Blackwell Publishers, 2001), 72.
19 David Robson, "Exponential Growth Bias: The Numerical Error behind Covid-19," *BBC Future*, August 12, 2020, https://www.bbc.com/future/article /20200812-exponential-growth-bias-the-numerical-error-behind-covid-19.
20 Gypsyamber D'Souza and David Dowdy, "Rethinking Herd Immunity and the Covid-19 Response End Game," John Hopkins University. Bloomberg School of Public Health, September 13, 2021, https://publichealth.jhu.edu/2021/what-is -herd-immunity-and-how-can-we-achieve-it-with-covid-19.
21 Gypsyamber D'Souza and David Dowdy, *op. cit.*
22 One might also ask what would happen if compliance with any norm could end up being "negotiated" – for example, the prohibition of theft, sexual abuse, or murder. It is worth noting from a comparative perspective how unthinkable such "negotiations" would be in contexts that do not require restricting social life with the use of masks, the limitation of mass gatherings, etc.
23 Giorgio Agamben, *Where We Are Now. The Epidemic as Politics* (New York and London: Rowman & Littlefield, 2021).

Bibliography

Agamben, Giorgio, *Where We Are Now. The Epidemic as Politics* (New York and London: Rowman and Littlefield, 2021).
Bachelard, Gaston, *The Formation of the Scientific Mind. A Contribution to the Psychoanalisis of Objective Knowledge* (Manchester: Clinamen, 2002 [1938]).
Bachelard, Gaston, *The New Scientific Spirit* (Boston: Beacon Press, 1985).
Baudrillard, Jean, *The Consumer Society* (Paris: Gallimard, 1970 [1998]).
Bauman, Zygmunt, *Community. Seeking Safety in an Insecure World* (Cambridge: Polity, 2001).
Beck, Ulrich, *Risk Society: Towards a New Modernity* (London and New York: Sage, 1992).
Berger, Peter and Luckmann, Thomas L., *The Social Construction of Reality. A Treatise in the Sociology of Knowledge* (New York: Doubleday, 1966).
Cohen, Stanley, *States of Denial: Knowing about Atrocities and Suffering* (Cambridge, UK: Blackwell Publishers, 2001).
Edelman, Marek, *The Ghetto Fights*. First published in Polish in Warsaw, 1945 (London: The Russell Press. 2013).
Feierstein, Daniel, "Political Violence in Argentina and its Genocidal Characteristics," *Journal of Genocide Research* 8, no. 2 (2006): 149–168, https://doi.org/10.1080 /14623520600703024.

Feierstein, Daniel, *Genocide as Social Practice. Reorganizing Society under Nazism and the Argentina Military Juntas* (New Jersey: Rutgers University Press, 2014).

Feierstein, Daniel, *Nuevos estudios sobre genocidio* (Mexico: Heredad, 2020).

Freud, Sigmund, "Formulations on the Two Principles of Mental Functioning" (1911), in *The Standard Edition of the Complete Psychological Works of Sigmund Freud* (London: The Hogarth Press and the Institute of Psycho-Analisis, 1958), Volume XII.

Freud, Sigmund, "Beyond the Pleasure Principle" (1920), in *The Standard Edition of the Complete Psychological Works of Sigmund Freud* (London: The Hogarth Press and the Institute of Psycho-Analisis, 1955), Volume XVIII.

Freud, Sigmund, "Negation," in *On Metapsychology, The Pelican Freud Library, vol. 11* (Harmondsworth: Penguin Books, 1977).

Grossman, Haika, *The Underground Army: Fighters of the Bialystok Ghetto* (New York: Holocaust Library, 1988).

Gruchoła, Małgorzata and Sławek-Czochra, Malgorzata, "The Culture of Fear" of Inhabitants of EU Countries in Their Reaction to the COVID-19 Pandemic – A Study Based on the Reports of the Eurobarometer," *Safety Science* 135 (2021), https://www.sciencedirect.com/science/article/pii/S0925753520305361.

Mannoni, Octave, *La otra escena. Claves de lo imaginario* (Buenos Aires: Amorrortu, 1979).

Piaget, Jean and García, Rolando, *Psychogenesis and the History of Science* (New York: Columbia University Press, 1989).

Preston, Paul, *The Spanish Holocaust: Inquisition and Extermination in Twentieth-Century Spain* (London: Harper Collins, 2012).

Puget, Janine and René Kaës (comp.), *Violencia de Estado y psicoanálisis* (Buenos Aires and México: Lumen, 2006).

Sartre, Jean-Paul, *Being and Nothingness: An Essay in Phenomenological Ontology*, translated by Sarah Richmond (Washington: First Washington Square Press/ Atria Paperback, 2021).

3 Projection, paranoia, and conspiracy theories during the COVID-19 crisis

Although the most common way of dealing with collective catastrophes is through denial, another defense mechanism also operates at the level of collective representations: projection. This mechanism is closely linked to hatred, as shown in Shakespeare's tragedy *Othello*, where Iago poisons Othello's imagination with jealousy, destroying his life and the lives of others around him. The Italian psychoanalyst Luigi Zoja has written, in a very provocative way, about that temptation in Shakespeare's work:

> Within ourselves, we must keep saying no to suspicion and allusion. For they are the real temptation, the only one that is constantly reborn. It is the evil that runs through each of us and the whole of history. For his part, he will keep tempting us, every day. For our part, we must say no to Iago.[1]

Jean Laplanche and Jean Bertrand Pontalis' *Language of Psychoanalysis* defines projection as the

> operation whereby qualities, feelings, wishes or even "objects," which the subject refuses to recognize or rejects in himself, are expelled from the self and located in another person or thing. Projection so understood is a defense of very primitive origin which may be seen at especially in paranoia, but also in "normal" modes of thought such as superstition.[2]

Freud consistently refers to the mechanism of projection in order to explain situations involving paranoia and phobias. A phobia is a persistent, excessive, unrealistic fear of an object, person, animal, activity, or situation. Freud believed that phobias originate in unresolved mental conflicts that are displaced or "projected" onto less threatening recipients such as dogs or elevators.

DOI: 10.4324/9781003267614-4

In paranoia, "the appeal to causality appears as an *a posteriori* rationalization of projection: [...] the proposition 'I hate him' becomes transformed by projection into another one: 'He hates (persecutes) me, which will justify me in hating him.'"[3] One dangerous aspect of paranoia, then, is that – unlike phobias – it can serve to legitimize violence toward others as "self-defense." In its malignant forms, paranoia is also a defense against self-harm. Laplanche and Pontalis suggest that whereas other mechanisms, such as denial or disavowal, are centered on "not wanting to know," projection adds to this "not wanting to be."

As we saw in the previous chapter, defense mechanisms are ways of coping with mental conflicts and tension. Projection, however, locates the undesirable feelings or emotions outside the individual so that they are perceived as an external threat. Freud explains this clearly in *Beyond the Pleasure Principle*:

> The excitations coming from within are, however, in their intensity and in other, qualitative, respects in their amplitude, perhaps more commensurate with the system's method of working than the stimuli which stream in from the external world. This state of things produces two definite results. First, the feelings of pleasure and unpleasure (which are an index to what is happening in the interior of the apparatus) predominate over all external stimuli. And secondly, a particular way is adopted of dealing with any internal excitations which produce too great an increase of unpleasure: there is a tendency to treat them as though they were acting, not from the inside, but from the outside, so that it may be possible to bring the shield against stimuli into operation as a means of defense against them. This is the origin of projection, which is destined to play such a large part in the causation of pathological processes.[4]

As we also saw in Chapter 2, the defense mechanisms of denial and disavowal form part of each individual's psychological make-up. Nevertheless, they find a parallel in collective representations based on pacts of denial and denialist rationalizations. We saw that these levels are interconnected in diverse and complex ways.

Like denial, individual projections (and in particular paranoia) may be linked to collective representations. The latter have their own logic, even though they too look for external explanations and causes of a malaise that comes *from within*. One author who has examined these collective representations closely is Luigi Zoja, in his book *Paranoia: The Madness That Makes History*.[5]

Although Zoja is careful to distinguish clinical paranoia and projection as a defense mechanism from paranoid frameworks for understanding the world, he uses the term "paranoia" for both levels of analysis. His argument for doing so is that: "By extension of the concept of clinical paranoia, I have adopted the term historico-cultural paranoia for a collective conviction based on wrong premises."[6] In other words, the concept (paranoia) and the system (conviction based on wrong premises) are the same at both levels, even if we need to distinguish between individual psychopathologies and collective representations.

Zoja adds that:

> The paranoiac feels the possibility of psychic collapse and defends himself [sic] against it by progressively simplifying his mental horizon, which is thus reduced to the dogma of absolute purity. On the collective level, the equivalent of this defense is the further transition from nationalism to racism.

Thus, racist ideologies and fundamentalist or exacerbated nationalisms function similarly to individual projections.

The difference between individual psychopathologies and collective representations is that in collective representations, the "dangerous other" is embodied in a social group rather than in another individual. Collective paranoia typically attempts to transfer the group's responsibility for some failure or wrongdoing onto a scapegoat in order to alleviate guilt or fear of punishment. At the same time, the scapegoat legitimizes the group's hatred of characteristics that group members are afraid to recognize in themselves. I have analyzed elsewhere how such mechanisms construct a "negative other" as a first and necessary step toward social segregation and exclusion and – in some cases – genocide.[7]

It is easy to see that scapegoating has also been used as an unconscious strategy to project the anguish and anxiety created by the COVID-19 pandemic. In most Western countries, the media have played a central role in the search for culprits. This approach has been accompanied by the diffusion of images intended to incite indignation and hatred.

In Argentina, a variety of groups were blamed for spreading the virus. These ranged from the so-called *runners*, who went jogging in Buenos Aires wooded parks, to the young people who flocked to the beaches during the summer of 2021. Similar groups were held responsible in Belgium, Italy, and Spain, among other countries. This search for "culprits" deflected the public's attention away from their own anguish and responsibility for the catastrophe.

In fact, most of us are unwilling to believe that the coronavirus is spread not only by what others do but by what we do ourselves. Projecting onto others simplifies the problem and transforms the discomfort and suffering created by the pandemic into hatred. This is the basic procedure used by fascist and neo-fascist groups to get people to disassociate from reality.[8]

Surveys carried out in Argentina showed that those who voted for opposition parties tended to blame the government for the spread of COVID-19 and subsequent deaths. At the same time, some complained – paradoxically – that lockdown restrictions were too severe. In contrast, government supporters tended to blame certain groups. Politics aside, it is necessary to distinguish general accusations against runners or young people from more specific accusations against those who explicitly organized "anti-quarantine marches." The latter explicitly opposed the government's health care measures and boycotted them in different ways. In this sense, it is particularly important to distinguish between scapegoats, who serve as targets of displaced aggression, and those people who are demonstrably to blame for spreading the pandemic.

And yet, however objective and unbiased accusations may be, one thing is glaringly obvious. Few people are willing to discuss their *own* responsibility for the spread of the virus. The question never arises because that is precisely how projection works: someone else is always to blame. Of course, this phenomenon is not exclusive to the COVID-19 pandemic. But the pandemic shows us how representations of reality can be constructed to alienate the individual from the social so that we do not have to think about the consequences of our actions.

In fact, it is true to say that projection is becoming more and more widespread as a strategy for dealing with anguish – and it does so by playing the blame game. This is linked to new forms of "desubjectivation." The positioning of whole populations as consumers and no longer as producers has led to a loss of identity and agency that has considerably reinforced projective strategies. We will return to this subject in greater depth in Chapter 4.

An endless stream of images of "others" that are "guilty" relieves us, then, of responsibility for our own carelessness. For despite media propaganda, family reunions, meetings with friends, and other indoor gatherings spread the coronavirus more surely than runners in parks or young people on beaches. This became clear in Argentina with the sharp increase in coronavirus infections during the first two weeks of January 2021 following the New Year celebrations. Interestingly, these cases proved independent of age, social class, or political leanings. Obviously, some individuals behaved less responsibly than others at New Year, but they did so as individuals rather than as groups.

In this sense, it is not possible to point the finger at "the young," "the old," "government supporters," "opposition supporters," or "poor people." It is true that *some* upper and upper-middle class travelers returning from abroad in March 2020 did not comply with the quarantine measures at the beginning of the pandemic. This spread the coronavirus around the city and province of Buenos Aires. It is also true that the following month, *some* members of the upper and upper-middle classes, ignoring lockdown, traveled to their vacation homes during Holy Week. But it would not be fair to blame a whole social class for spreading the virus to the wider population. Most well-to-do Argentineans probably did obey the rules and, in any case, the working class and the poor cannot afford second homes or trips to Europe. Except for the most radical anti-quarantine and "libertarian" groups who systematically tried to boycott public health measures, not even political convictions played a significant role.

As we saw earlier, blaming a group to which we do not belong relieves our feelings of guilt and allows us to get rid of our hatred, anger, and anguish. We project them onto a scapegoat. For middle-aged and middle class Argentineans, the "usual suspects" of any sort of criminal activity are generally young people and/or the inhabitants of poor neighborhoods. They are the ideal scapegoats.

Elsewhere, there were several attempts at the beginning of the pandemic to direct hatred toward other populations. First, it was the Chinese, for having "invented" the pandemic; then, the Jews, for having created a conspiracy to dominate the rest of humanity through the virus. It was not clear what such a conspiracy consisted of or how the Jews could have used it to their advantage. Nevertheless, the accusations persisted.

Giorgio Agamben and other "progressive" conspiracy theorists even attributed responsibility for the pandemic to a group of wicked and anonymous illuminati supposedly operating behind the scenes to "override our wishes." As we shall see later in this chapter, the notion of freedom as "freedom to do as I wish" is a formidable strategy of political domination. It sweeps away nobler feelings such as modesty, shame, and guilt that recognize the rights of others and the harm we may be doing to them.

Traditionally, psychological disorders have been divided into psychoses and neuroses. A neurosis may affect a person's relationships, ability to work, and general wellbeing, but the sufferer does not lose touch with reality. On the other hand, the main symptoms of psychosis are hallucinations and delusions. At the clinical level, paranoia typically involves hostile beliefs about others, while at the level of representations, paranoid projections tend to lead to violence in one form or another.

History offers many examples of ethnic, political, or religious groups being blamed unjustly for natural or social catastrophes. These groups have suffered more or less spontaneous aggression in the form of pogroms, lynchings, burning of homes, expulsions, deportations, as well as politically-motivated state persecution such as that perpetrated by the Nazis.

Nazi ideology was based on the myth that Germany did not lose the First World War on the battlefield but because civilians, especially Jews and communists, had undermined the war effort on the home front.

In fact, the "stab in the back" is a classic paranoid motif. At the beginning of the 20th century, Turkish nationalists blamed the Armenian population for the misfortunes and the increasing disintegration of the Ottoman Empire. Eighty years later, myths about the 15th-century Christian–Muslim battles were revived in former Yugoslavia to explain the crises of the late 20th century. Here, the Bosnian populations were depicted as the "treacherous" heirs of the "Muslim invaders." More generally, beneath the political or religious ideologies that underpin and legitimize persecution, we always find some sort of paranoid projection. Except for the colonial devaluing of indigenous peoples, this has been true of all forms of dehumanization throughout history.

Fortunately, such images and accusations have not yet taken hold in relation to the pandemic. Between January and March 2020, there were a number of attacks against Asians in Europe and America, but these were isolated incidents. However, a rapid increase in more extreme forms of projection can by no means be ruled out if strategies for dealing with the pandemic continue to fail or if the infection and death rates continue to rise. This scenario could easily appear if random mutations that occur during the global transmission of the virus become more contagious or more lethal.

Zoja understands aggressive nationalism and the racism to which it often gives rise as collective forms of social paranoia:

> The racist argument confuses the order of events. His arguments lack consequentiality, being produced not by observation of the facts, but by a pre-existing unconscious need. It is this that makes them almost ineradicable. Racism is always paranoid, and *there are no preventive medicines against paranoia*; it is already convinced that is the prevention of preventions.[9]

This is how he describes the way it functions:

> We have seen that a constant feature of false paranoid reasoning is circularity: instead of formulating a real thought, it thinks it is advancing at the very time when it is retracing its steps. It expresses itself in tautologies; it repeats what it said at the outset, merely changing the formulation.[10]

With respect to the COVID-19 pandemic, conspiracy theories have – until now – been embraced mainly by the neo-fascist right. Nevertheless, they have circulated rapidly both in Europe (France, Germany, Italy, Hungary, and Poland) and in the United States, Brazil, and other Latin American countries. Conspiracy theorists argue that the coronavirus is an invention of international organizations such as the World Health Organization and the media. Its purpose is to keep us locked up and to discipline us so that we cannot fulfill our wishes. Who would stand to gain politically or economically from such a measure is not clear. According to some versions of the conspiracy theory, the Big Pharma companies would profit from selling vaccines; according to others, governments would have an excuse to crack down on political opponents by suspending parliamentary institutions or on the population as a whole by declaring a state of emergency.

The more extreme forms of paranoia suggest (though never explicitly state) that the conspirators secretly indulge in everything they have forbidden to others. This suspicion was fueled in Argentina and other Latin American countries by reports (and later photographs and videos) of dinner parties and barbecues organized by the Argentine president and other public officials that violated the quarantine restrictions decreed by the president himself. The same happened in 2021 and 2022 in the UK and other European countries. This goes to show that during lockdown and other national crises politicians *must* lead by example. Double standards simply reinforce our latent paranoia by (apparently) confirming our worst fears.

In some cases, growing paranoia has led to hatred and rebellion against public health measures. This has included not only the public burning of face masks but also threats against health workers and high-profile scientists. In Germany, the situation became worrying after the Robert Koch Institute, the main public health advisory body to the German government, received hundreds of emails threatening its scientists at the end of 2020. The building itself was attacked with Molotov cocktails in October 2020 although fortunately no one was injured and a security guard was quick to extinguish the flames. In Germany, too, virologist Christian Drosten received death threats for advocating restrictions in social areas such as schools and kindergartens. Further incidents have included anti-vaxxer demonstrators wearing yellow stars and chanting "vaccination makes you free" in an attempt to compare COVID-19 restrictions with the Nazi persecution of the Jews.[11]

Similar situations have arisen in Argentina, although they have received less media attention. Public health workers were scapegoated at the beginning of the pandemic and scientists, such as infectologist Gabriela Piovano, were harassed at the start of 2021. These behaviors reflect a particularly problematic combination of projection and paranoid delusion and constitute a serious breakdown of social cohesion.

Those who take part in such actions are paradoxically convinced of the soundness of their arguments. It is the strength of these arguments that allows them to project their anguish, anger, impotence, or hatred against an explicit enemy: governments and scientists who announce what these groups of people do not want to hear. What they do not want to hear – what triggers their denial, projections, and paranoia – is the intrusion of death into their everyday lives. It is also the abrupt transformation of daily life, including restrictions on movement involving significant economic and social suffering, and the need to postpone gratification. The latter is something that the dominant socio-economic system based on permanently fueling demand and consumption has constructed as undesirable and even impossible.

We can find softer forms of projection in the ever more frequent accusations of "moralizing" whenever someone mentions the need for public health measures that are not "voluntarily negotiated." Such measures, of course, limit our personal freedom not only to protect us but also to protect others. In Western societies, however, appeals to behave pro-socially have become unacceptable unless they involve property. Consequently, those who complain about "moralizing" are really trying to justify a "business as usual" or "carry on regardless" attitude. They are unable to understand that the only way to confront a catastrophe that has turned our world upside down is by changing everybody's social behavior.

In this sense, even the analogy with AIDS (which is so useful in the sociology of health for thinking about harm reduction strategies) becomes problematic. COVID-19 is not a sexually transmitted disease but an airborne one. This gives it a much higher level of contagiousness but above all makes certain activities unfeasible, such as gatherings of large numbers of people in enclosed spaces. The concept of "safe sex" that allowed the fight against AIDS has no analogy here since there are no "safe" ways for large groups of people to gather in enclosed places. Consequently, certain behaviors must be eliminated altogether until the community transmission of the virus has been eradicated. Trying to come up with "protocols" for activities that cannot be protocoled is simply another form of denial – an attempt to postpone the inevitable. Instead, we must accept the need to make changes in our lives.

To further illustrate the sort of misinformed opinions that I have just mentioned, let us look at a newspaper article published in Argentina by María Pía López, a sociologist. The article argues that we can all behave responsibly during the pandemic without having to make sacrifices. On the subject of school excursions, López claims that "the end-of-year trip is an expected rite, an announced enjoyment, a rite of passage" and that its "prohibition" would generate effects similar to those of prohibiting abortion or sex in the case of AIDS. She demands "protected" excursions equivalent to "safe sex" or "safe abortion."

The problem of arguing by analogy is clear. In order to reintroduce those end-of-course trips later on, it is first necessary to eliminate large community transmission of the virus. This means suspending mass events in enclosed spaces, including end-of-course trips involving mass transportation and indoor gatherings. López's refusal to accept that there can be no end-of-year trips for some time (for example, just in 2020) simply leads to more denial, which continued to spread the virus in moments of important community transmission.

At present, it seems that airborne pandemics can only be stopped by mass vaccination. Otherwise, movements and close contact between people must be restricted as much as possible. In fact, containment strategies, including attempts to trace and isolate those infected, allowed people in many countries, such as China, Australia, Norway, South Korea, and Singapore to resume nearly all their previous activities during most of 2020 and 2021.

As long as people refuse to postpone gratification, the virus will continue to circulate and people will believe they are reducing the harm caused by the pandemic when in fact they are making it worse. Their confusion arises from an inability to distinguish what is temporary from what is permanent. It is not that the end-of-year trip or any other social occasion we miss will "never" return. It is simply that sometimes we must wait until public health measures have been successful. The more we resist these restrictions, the longer they will be necessary. The SARS-COV-2 virus does not live more than 20 days, but unless we can accept and comply with restrictions for 20 days, the virus will continue to circulate and new restrictions will become necessary later on. This is a fundamental difference between an airborne and a sexually transmitted disease.

As mentioned in Chapter 1, thinking develops through analogies. But faulty analogies can obscure and block our understanding of a situation. A useful analogy requires detailed knowledge of both sides of the comparison in order to distinguish which elements are similar and which are not. It is not enough to appeal to catch-all phrases or "mantras" (e.g. harm reduction, "negotiation" of the rules, etc.); these must be adapted to take into account the differences between the situations under analysis.

In trying to understand the reality of the pandemic, one of the greatest challenges for any discipline is to distinguish useful analogies from those that hold us back and to fine-tune these analogies at any given moment. For this, there is no alternative to a transdisciplinary approach. Unlike multidisciplinarity and interdisciplinarity, transdisciplinary research is open to very different epistemological perspectives from the social and natural sciences and integrates more real-world actors and data than traditional academic approaches.

The search for self-preservation

Projection is often entangled in different ways with denial. Paradoxically, denying the existence of a phenomenon like the COVID-19 pandemic and making someone else responsible for it are not mutually exclusive positions. A public and notorious example of this sort of inconsistency can be found in former US President Donald Trump. Trump denied the existence of the COVID-19 pandemic ("it is a flu; it will go away; the WHO is exaggerating and is wrong; the virus will not reach the United States; the situation is under control") and simultaneously blamed the Chinese for it. He not only called it the "Chinese virus" but repeatedly accused China of creating and spreading it.

The main factor underlying these contradictory beliefs is the instinct of self-preservation – the will to live. Survivors of Nazi concentration and extermination camps not only complained about denial, they also described with sadness and pain the omnipresence of projection, which they attributed to the difficulty of accepting one's own imminent death. This conclusion that could also be drawn from any more or less critical analysis of Nazi policies in the occupied territories. Let us see now what this analogy between the pandemic and the Nazi persecutions can tell us, while remaining clear about which levels of this analogy are relevant and which are not.

It is Marek Edelman who provides one of the most forceful descriptions of how these elements played out:

> The instinct for self-preservation finally drove the people into a state of mind permitting them to disregard the safety of others in order to save their own necks. True, nobody as yet believed that the deportation meant death. But the Germans had already succeeded in dividing the Jewish population into two distinct groups – those already condemned to die and those who still hoped to remain alive. Afterwards, step by step, the Germans succeeded in pitting these two groups one against another and occasionally caused some Jews to lead others to certain death in order to save their own skin.[12]

A clear example of people sacrificing others to save themselves can be found in many of the Jewish councils (Judenräte) imposed by the Nazis on Jewish communities across occupied Europe. Often the Judenräte collaborated with the German authorities in selecting victims for deportation. The victims were then rounded up by the Jewish police and delivered to the Nazis.[13]

The instinct of self-preservation led to unusual forms of self-deception, which projected extermination onto "other Jews." Haika Grossman ironized with her comrades of the Jewish resistance that each of the millions of Jews in denial believed they could be one of the four or five Jews that Hitler would parade in his museums as examples of an annihilated culture.[14]

Perhaps one of the most heartbreaking stories of denial and projection is Shmerke Kaczerginski's account of the death of Yitzhak Wittenberg, the resistance commander of the Vilna ghetto.[15] Wittenberg was arrested by Lithuanian police during a meeting of the Vilna Judenrat after the head of the ghetto authority betrayed him to the Gestapo. Suspecting this might happen, resistance fighters attacked the police on the way to the prison and freed Wittenberg, who went underground in sectors of the ghetto to which neither the Jewish police nor German troops had access. Here, armed sectors of the resistance were in hiding, ready to sell their lives dearly.

Instead of seeking direct armed confrontation with the Jewish resistance, the Nazis decided to break the will of the population to fight by implementing "collective responsibility." They threatened the Judenrat with daily deportations if the authorities and the population at large did not find and hand over the head of the resistance alive so that he could be interrogated by the German security forces.

The Nazis thus used the Jewish council to win the dispute for hearts and minds in the streets of the Vilna ghetto. Many of the ghetto inhabitants confronted the members of the resistance with the cry "we want to live," demanding that Wittenberg turn himself in. The resistance was faced with the dilemma of firing on the Jewish population or giving in to their demand to hand over their commander.

Finally, the unified command of the Jewish resistance groups decided to surrender Wittenberg in order to avoid a fratricidal struggle with the Jewish police and desperate crowds of ghetto inhabitants. Wittenberg considered suicide to avoid the fate the Gestapo had in store for him, but the Nazis wanted him alive. Wittenberg finally agreed, showing great heroism in the face of those who sought to exchange his life for their own. Some say that in prison, Wittenberg died under torture; others claim that he took poison and was found dead in his cell the following morning.

The Vilna ghetto was liquidated only a few months later with barely token resistance. The best fighters had fled to the forests after the "Wittenberg case," deeply disappointed by their fellow Jews who had sunk into moral depravity in order to maintain the hope of survival until the end.[16]

Despite the obvious differences between the COVID-19 pandemic and the Nazi genocide, what this story illustrates is how our wish to live can act as an "epistemological obstacle," blinding us to reality. Denial and projection prevent us having to face the possibility of our own death and that of our loved ones. The story also illustrates how our instinct for self-preservation can undo any strategy to face the catastrophe once fear has triggered an every-man-for-himself response. Without social solidarity and political organization, individual salvation in situations like these is a flight to nowhere. In the Vilna ghetto the whole population was deported. In the COVID-19 pandemic, the virus will eventually reach every family if community transmission is not stopped, no matter how many lies we tell ourselves.

To put it another way, an every-man-for-himself response constructs *other people* as the enemy – or at least the problem. This makes it impossible to coordinate any sort of collective action other than returning to life as it was before the catastrophe. Clinging to the notion of "business as usual," however, puts everyone's life at risk and reduces the chances of returning to normal in the future.

Nevertheless, decades of hyper-individualism and praise for the self-made man (as embodied in the entrepreneur) have made a deep impression on our contemporary subjectivity. They are behind the insistence on freedoms at a time when we should be thinking more about responsibilities. This is true not only of those who identify as liberals but those who see themselves as progressives. We will examine this point in more detail in Chapter 4, which considers the ethical and political dilemmas raised by the pandemic.

While the COVID-19 pandemic is different, then, from the systematic extermination of the Jews during the so-called "final solution," the analogy may serve to illustrate how denial and projection operate in extreme circumstances. It is possible that our instinct for self-preservation is blinding many of us to the nature of this new virus, its high level of contagiousness, virulence, and possible sequelae. If this is true, it will be very difficult to persuade the community to take appropriate preventive measures.

The Nazi occupation forced the inhabitants of the Vilna ghetto to focus on survival. In contrast, since the COVID-19 crisis began, many people have been clinging not so much to life itself as to memories of their previous lives. They have not yet managed to mourn the necessary (albeit temporary) interruption of normal activities. Together with a tremendous difficulty in accepting any form of postponement, this inability to grieve has been instrumental in the appearance of denial and projection during the pandemic. It is probably true to say that the struggle has been not only to survive but to preserve identity and that these two goals have often been in conflict with one another.

Shame and guilt

Guilt involves feeling remorse for something specific we have done. Shame, on the other hand, is the feeling that our whole self is wrong. Shame may be related to other people's opinions rather than to a specific behavior or event and, when this is true, it may impact negatively on our interpersonal relationships.[17] I would like to make it clear, then, that I am using the term in Zoja's sense of an *instinctive* sense of right and wrong that compels us to face our responsibilities to others rather than the urge to deny or escape the shame-inducing situation.[18,19]

Over the last century or so, guilt and shame have lost much of their former power. The modern rebellion against tradition and the postmodern rebellion against "grand narratives" have largely made such feelings (once highly valued) a thing of the past. Nowadays, shame and guilt are seen only as tools of domination. This is because they were once used by secular and religious leaders to impose the worldview of the powerful and maintain social order – often in the name of a judgmental God who handed down condemnation. In the modern world, these emotions are considered to be a sign that someone is afraid of their desires.

In many ways, of course, rebellion against tradition and authority has been liberating. But this tells only half the story since shame and guilt have given rise to very different forms of representation beyond the use made of them by the ruling elites. Indeed, our rejection of such feelings has also proved functional to the contemporary order of domination. Power is no longer vested in moralizing religions or a prayerful examination of one's conscience (except in very specific cases such as Christian and Jewish fundamentalist movements and some Islamic countries) but rather in the ability to manipulate the consumer. The "sacredness" of freedom is invoked to overcome any objective or subjective obstacle to making money, including one's own and others' moral qualms.

The Dominican priest Jean Baptiste Lacordaire synthesized this idea clearly at the beginning of the 19th century: "Between the strong and the weak, between the rich and the poor, between the master and the servant, it is freedom that oppresses and the law that redeems."[20] Hence, the term "moralizing," which in earlier centuries held positive connotations, is now a term of contempt used to legitimize the hegemonic exercise of power in the 21st century.

A growing skepticism about moral responsibility has been accompanied by an increasing unwillingness to judge blameworthiness (or praiseworthiness). This is true whether judgment is on-going or final and whether it involves self-judgment, as in the Jewish Day of Atonement, judgment by ancestors (as in some African, Australian, and Melanesian cultures), or judgment by an omnipotent God. At the same time, we have blunted our critical faculties – our ability to distinguish right from wrong – by confusing morality in a broad sense with the conventional moral restraints of the past. Rejecting these restraints has not led to a new counterhegemonic morality or a more equitable society. On the contrary, it has constructed freedom and desire as the only grounds for action, and any appeal to moral responsibility as an unjustifiable intrusion.

Contemporary attitudes to shame and guilt show a tendency toward oversimplification and improvisation. It is true that in the past shame and guilt were closely linked to political and social control. Confession in the Catholic Church is a clear example. But we have now gone to the opposite extreme, where those who challenge selfishness and hedonism as the basis of behavior in this era of financial capitalism are accused of "moralizing." No one is interested in making a true confession anymore; instead, they are concerned about protecting their actions from scrutiny and criticism.

The idea that discipline continues to be the main tool of social control and domination (as Michel Foucault claimed in the 1960s and 1970s) ignores the changes that have occurred since the end of the 20th century. Nowadays, power is linked more to the ability to manipulate people's desires than to Victorian-style repression and taboos. Foucault himself had already noticed this trend in what he called the *obligation* to "talk about sex" that appeared in the second half of the 20th century as the reverse side of a previous prohibition.[21]

Let us now return to Zoja for a deeper reflection on the role of shame:

> Shame is a very simple feeling and, if it is not manipulated from above, restores a simple justice in social relations: it corresponds to an instinctive self-criticism for having disturbed the rules – *mores*, whence "morality" – of society. This potential for self-criticism, which does not require any particular intellectual training, is inherent in us from birth.[22]

Indeed, as Silvia Bleichmar points out, modesty and shame are basic responses to the presence of others.[23] To be ashamed is to recognize that my actions may cause discomfort to others and perhaps even harm. But that is not all. Shame and embarrassment alert me to the fact that the discomfort or harm I have caused can damage my relationships with others. To repair these relationships, it may not be enough to stop causing the discomfort or harm; I may have to offer reparation for the suffering I have inflicted. Being ashamed of my behavior can give rise to self-criticism, a fundamental opportunity to confront denial, projection, and paranoid ways of thinking.

Shame can allow me to accept the evil that resides in me, consciously or unconsciously. I may harm others intentionally, or by treating them as mere objects, or by hoarding a scarce resource for my own enjoyment. In the case of a pandemic, I may expose a third party to the risk of infection as a result of my own selfish behavior.

As June Price Tangney and Ronda L. Dearing point out, "[s]hame is focused on a failing in the self ('Look what *I*'ve done'), but guilt focuses on morally disappointing behavior ('Look what I've *done*')."[24] The transformation of shame into guilt generally leads to a desire to make amends and finds expression in new representations of reality. Guilt implies not only an internal awareness and acceptance of shame but also the need to respond to one's actions. Responsibility is the ability and willingness to respond or answer to others for what we have done and to put right what we are ashamed of.

We see, then, that feelings and representations are interconnected and are capable of influencing behavior. First, an almost physical response (modesty) is accompanied by a basic emotion (shame); this feeling is then accepted and given a meaning by the subject (guilt), making it possible to act in response to the feeling and also creating a framework of representation in which to do so: responsibility.

Thanks to the modern and postmodern belittling of shame and guilt and the relativizing of responsibility, we now live in communities of increasingly irresponsible individualism. I use the word "irresponsible" not as an insult but in a descriptive sense to denote individuals who often do not perceive the discomfort or harm they cause others and – even if they do – are increasingly incapable of feeling shame and guilt and so make no effort to change their behavior. This lack of responsibility lies at the root of many contemporary social problems and mental disorders.

We live in a world organized around self-help, where we are responsible only to and for ourselves, and victim playing, where it is always others who must compensate us for present or past injustices – never the other way round. We are all experts at inventing or exaggerating victimhood to seek attention and/or manipulate others. But victimhood seems to relieve us from any obligation to others or any possible feelings of shame or guilt. It is a wonderful facilitator of projection. Once we cast ourselves in the role of victims, we necessarily cast others in the role of victimizers and the cause of all our suffering. When this situation is multiplied to infinity, it can only lead to violence and a proliferation of projection and paranoia.

Without shame and guilt, our worst passions will develop unfettered. We have seen this in much of the Western world in the very limited cooperation and solidarity shown in response to the COVID-19 pandemic. However, the same indifference has characterized our response to a whole series of social and natural disasters in recent decades – catastrophes such as wars, earthquakes, tsunamis, floods, and droughts. It is no coincidence that the COVID-19 virus has been much more effectively contained in Asian societies where guilt and shame still play an important role in individual subjectivity and are linked to notions of social responsibility.

We may be confused by accusations of authoritarian government and lack of freedom in countries like China, Thailand, or Vietnam. But democracies such as South Korea – and Australia and Norway for that matter – also managed to implement strict quarantine measures. Their citizens understood the need for rules to protect themselves and others, and presumably felt shame and guilt when tempted to break the rules. It is difficult to explain the success of these countries in containing the pandemic through repressive measures alone, especially as there was no significant increase in state persecution in most of these countries during the pandemic. It is true that some countries (especially China) are increasingly using mass surveillance to monitor their citizens. However, this cannot have been the only factor in preventing community transmission of the virus since police repression alone would not have been enough to stop people coming into contact with one another.

A rigorous analysis of shame, guilt, and responsibility may provide tools that not only help us understand the pandemic but also how social behaviors and social relations are being transformed in this new century. Once again, we turn to Luigi Zoja for an insight into the "contagious" nature of social behavior – especially evil:

> The hope – not an impossible one – is that this shame may be the antithesis of evil infection: if not a direct "contagion of goodness," which unfortunately is not as infectious as evil, at least a step towards greater awareness. How simple life would be if crimes were always conscious choices. Evil is mainly contagion, psychic infection. It may be an unconscious lack of moral conscience.[25]

Nevertheless, even though denial, projection, and paranoia are highly contagious, perhaps some forms of responsibility could re-emerge to neutralize them if we made room for shame and guilt. The question is whether we are willing to after almost half a century of mockery and disparagement that have paradoxically left us feeling ashamed and guilty for feeling shame and guilt, and despising those emotions that could make us better people.

In recent decades, we have created societies that encourage our worst tendencies – denial, willful blindness, playing the victim, projection, and paranoia. But all these are produced by human action, the same as shame, guilt, and responsibility. Here I would like to emphasize that guilt means taking responsibility for our actions; it is not the feeling of being blamed. The blame game is rampant in the 21st century as a projection strategy, but it does not improve our critical thinking and problem-solving abilities or our ability to empathize with others. It is simply an excuse to unleash our worst demons onto others.

Before ending this chapter, I would like to enumerate a few broad questions arising from the COVID-19 pandemic. For example, is it possible to make a critical balance of present-day society in terms of individual subjectivities starting from our experience of the pandemic? Are we ready make an honest appraisal of our weaknesses as well as our strengths in the ways we respond to complex social challenges? What triumphs and defeats have we experienced? What lessons can we draw?

As social and political agents, we not only need to understand our world, we also need to assess our chances of improving it. Of course, we must do so without deceiving ourselves but, at the same time, without losing hope. If the purpose of knowledge is action, then we can surely organize our knowledge in future according to the actions possible in a given event and the way in which these actions are interconnected.

In the previous chapters we examined the different public health measures that have been implemented since the outbreak of the current pandemic – with some examples in Argentina – and the reasons why they succeeded or – more often – failed. In Chapter 4 we will consider the consequences of these successes and failures for dealing with the catastrophes and crises to come in this brave new world we are building.

Notes

1   Luigi Zoja, *Paranoia: The Madness That Makes History* (London and New York: Routledge, 2017), 322.
2   Jean Laplanche and Jean-Bertrand Pontalis, *The Language of Psycho-Analysis*, translated by Donald Nicholson-Smith (London: Karnak, 1973), 349.
3   Ibid., 353.
4   Sigmund Freud, *Beyond the Pleasure Principle*, translated and edited by James Strachey (New York: Norton, 1961), 23.
5   Luigi Zoja, *Paranoia: The Madness that Makes History* (London and New York: Routledge, 2017).
6   Ibid., 87.
7   See for example Chapter 6 of Daniel Feierstein, *Genocide as Social Practice: Reorganizing Society under the Nazis and Argentina's Military Juntas* (New Jersey: Rutgers University Press, 2014).
8   For a detailed discussion of how paranoid representations are constructed, see Daniel Feierstein, *La construcción del enano fascista. Los usos del odio como estrategia política en Argentina* (Buenos Aires: Capital Intelectual, 2020).
9   Luigi Zoja, *op. cit.*, 147–148.
10 Ibid., 299.
11 See, for example, "Angriff auf Gebäude des Robert Koch-Instituts," on aerzteblatt.de, October 26, 2020, available online: https://www.aerzteblatt.de/nach-richten/117716/Angriff-auf-Gebaeude-des-Robert-Koch-Instituts;   "Virologe

Drosten Erhalte Morddrohungen," on aerzteblatt.de, April 27, 2020, available online: https://www.aerzteblatt.de/nachrichten/112358/Virologe-Drosten -Erhalte-Morddrohungen; and "Auf Corona-Demos. Klein verurteilt Judenstern-Kopien," on ZDF, May 21, 2020, available online: https://www.zdf.de/nach-richten/politik/corona-demos-klein-judenstern-kopien-100.html. I thank my sister Liliana Feierstein for keeping me up to date on the situation in Germany and sending me numerous materials on the subject.

12 Marek Edelman, *The Ghetto Fights*. First published in Polish in Warsaw, 1945 (London: The Russell Press, 2013), 40.

13 The different policies implemented by the different Judenräte have been analyzed in depth by Isaiah Trunk in *Judenrat. The Jewish Councils in Eastern Europe under Nazi Occupation* (Lincoln: University of Nebraska Press, 1996).

14 See Haika Grossman, *The Underground Army: Fighters of the Bialystok Ghetto* (Holocaust Library, 1988).

15 Shmerke Kaczerginski, *Memoirs of a Jewish Guerilla Fighter* (Hebrew) (Tel Aviv, 1980). This book is published in Spanish as Shmerke Kaczerginski, *Diario de un guerrillero* (Buenos Aires, Milá, 1989).

16 The Wittenberg case has been discussed in depth in Daniel Feierstein; "The Dilemma of Wittenberg: Analysis of Tactics and Ethics," Shofar (*Journal of Jewish Social Studies*), University of Nebraska Press, Vol. 20.2, 2002, while a comparative analysis of the politics of resistance can be found in Daniel Feierstein, "The Jewish Resistance Movements in the Ghettos of Eastern Europe: Reflections on the Relationships of Force" (trad. Steven Sadow), in *Life in the Ghettos during the Holocaust*, edited by Eric Sterling (Syracuse: Syracuse University Press, 2005), 220–257.

17 June Price Tangney and Ronda L. Dearing, *Shame and Guilt* (New York: The Guilford Press, 2002).

18 Tangney and Dearing, *op. cit.*

19 Luigi Zoja, *op. cit.*, 280.

20 "Entre le fort et le faible, entre le riche et le pauvre, entre le maître et le serviteur, c'est la liberté qui opprime et la loi qui affranchit." Lacordaire, Henri Dominique (1872). *Conférences de Notre-Dame de Paris: Années 1846–1848, Volume 3*. Google books: Poussielgue frères, 473.

21 Michel Foucault, *The History of Sexuality Volume 1: An Introduction* (London: Allen Lane, 1979 [1976]).

22 Luigi Zoja, *op. cit.*, 280.

23 Silvia Bleichmar, *Vergüenza, culpa y pudor* (Buenos Aires: Paidós, 2016).

24 Tangney and Dearing, *op. cit.*, ix.

25 Luigi Zoja, *op. cit.*, 280.

Bibliography

Bachelard, Gaston, *The Formation of the Scientific Mind. A Contribution to the Psychoanalisis of Objective Knowledge* (Manchester: Clinamen, 2002 [1938]).

Baudrillard, Jean, *The Consumer Society* (Paris: Gallimard, 1970 [1998]).

Bauman, Zygmunt, *Community. Seeking Safety in an Insecure World* (Cambridge: Polity, 2001).

Beck, Ulrich, *Risk Society: Towards a New Modernity* (London and New York: Sage, 1992).

Berger, Peter and Luckmann, Thomas L., *The Social Construction of Reality. A Treatise in the Sociology of Knowledge* (New York: Doubleday, 1966).

Bleichmar, Silvia, *Vergüenza, culpa y pudor* (Buenos Aires: Paidós, 2016).

Cohen, Stanley, *States of Denial: Knowing about Atrocities and Suffering* (Cambridge, UK: Blackwell Publishers, 2001).

Edelman, Marek, *The Ghetto Fights*. First published in Polish in Warsaw, 1945 (London: The Russell Press, 2013).

Feierstein, Daniel, "The Dilemma of Wittenberg: Analysis of Tactics and Ethics," *Shofar (Journal of Jewish Social Studies)*, University of Nebraska Press, 20, no. 2 (2002). pp (61–68).

Feierstein, Daniel, "Political Violence in Argentina and its Genocidal Characteristics," *Journal of Genocide Research* 8, no. 2 (2006): 149–168, https://doi.org/10.1080/14623520600703024.

Feierstein, Daniel, *Genocide as Social Practice. Reorganizing Society under Nazism and the Argentina Military Juntas* (New Jersey: Rutgers University Press, 2014).

Feierstein, Daniel, *La construcción del enano fascista. Los usos del odio como estrategia política en Argentina* (Buenos Aires: Capital Intelectual, 2020).

Foucault, Michel, *The History of Sexuality Volume 1: An Introduction* (London: Allen Lane, 1979 [1976]).

Freud, Sigmund, "Formulations on the Two Principles of Mental Functioning" (1911), in *The Standard Edition of the Complete Psychological Works of Sigmund Freud* (London: The Hogarth Press and the Institute of Psycho-Analisis, 1958) Volume XII.

Freud, Sigmund, "Beyond the Pleasure Principle" (1920), in *The Standard Edition of the Complete Psychological Works of Sigmund Freud* (London: The Hogarth Press and the Institute of Psycho-Analisis, 1955), Volume XVIII.

Grossman, Haika, *The Underground Army: Fighters of the Bialystok Ghetto* (New York: Holocaust Library, 1988).

Kaczerginski, Shmerke, *Memoirs of a Jewish Guerilla Fighter* (Hebrew) (Tel Aviv, 1980). This book is published in Spanish as Shmerke Kaczerginski, *Diario de un guerrillero* (Buenos Aires: Milá, 1989).

Laplanche, Jean and Jean-Bertrand Pontalis, *The Language of Psycho-Analysis*, trans. Donald Nicholson-Smith (London: Karnak, 1973).

Puget, Janine and René Kaës (comp.), *Violencia de Estado y psicoanálisis* (Buenos Aires and México: Lumen, 2006).

Sterling, Eric (ed.), *Life in the Ghettos during the Holocaust* (Syracuse, New York: Syracuse University Press, 2005).

Tangney, June Price and Ronda L. Dearing, *Shame and Guilt* (New York: The Guilford Press, 2002).

Trunk, Isaiah, *Judenrat. The Jewish Councils in Eastern Europe under Nazi Occupation* (Lincoln: University of Nebraska Press, 1996).

Zoja, Luigi, *Paranoia: The Madness that Makes History* (London and New York: Routledge, 2017).

4 Taking stock of the crisis of COVID-19

The COVID-19 crisis has confirmed the lessons learned from other pandemics, most notably the Spanish flu of a century ago. Societies that follow the precautionary principle and impose strict public health measures during an airborne infectious disease outbreak save more lives and rescue their economies faster than those that do not. Strict measures lasting several weeks or months actually make it possible to restore normal freedoms and social life more quickly than half-measures or restrictions that are lifted before the virus has been eradicated.

However, the current pandemic has also shown how effective community responses to social problems are hindered by the current consumerist culture, which values individualism and immediate satisfaction over moral concern for others. Indeed, many members of society nowadays cast themselves in the role of victims, childishly demanding "rights" from public institutions while avoiding responsibilities. This gradual diffusion of responsibility is linked to a growing emphasis on citizens as consumers rather than producers. Unable to accept temporary controls, societies paradoxically end up paying a much higher price when faced with crises like the COVID-19 pandemic.

The circular relationship between new forms of individual subjectivity and social organization has simply consolidated power elites at the expense of social solidarity. The pandemic has illustrated the devastating consequences of liberal individualism during a catastrophe.

Fortunately, some of the worst predictions about the COVID-19 crisis have not so far come true. For instance:

1) The virus is not as deadly as it seemed in the first months, but it has turned out to be much deadlier than influenza, with which it was originally compared. In 2020–2021, the COVID infection fatality ratio has been around 0.1 to 0.3 percent per year in countries that have allowed the virus to spread, such as Argentina, Brazil, Italy, Mexico, the United

DOI: 10.4324/9781003267614-5

Kingdom, and the United States. The COVID-19 virus has been particularly severe and fatal in certain groups – for example, people over 60 years of age or those with respiratory problems, heart disease, and/or diabetes, among others. Nevertheless, the new variants have proved more serious in younger groups (including young adults) and those without comorbidities.

2) Natural immunity to the COVID-19 virus has not developed in any society. In May–June 2020, it was expected that 10–20 percent would become immune, and this prediction increased to 50–60 percent at the beginning of 2021. Neither of these expectations has been met.

3) It has been confirmed that COVID-19 is an airborne virus (which explains the speed at which it spreads). People without symptoms can have viral loads as high as those with symptoms and can spread the virus without knowing they are infected. This must be a key factor to consider in policy making. It also means that children are an important vehicle of community transmission of the virus, a fact denied for almost a year in many Western nations.

At the time of writing, several important questions remain unanswered, such as the long-term sequelae in COVID-19 patients;[1] whether these sequelae occur only in severe cases or also in mild and asymptomatic cases; the risk of reinfection both from the same variant and different mutations; and the severity of reinfections in comparison to the original infection. Also, the behavior and effects of the different mutations and variants of the virus are not well understood. It is difficult to predict how the virus will evolve or whether the available COVID-19 vaccines will retain their currently high level of effectiveness.

What the future holds in store, then, remains unknown. It is true that several vaccines appear to be effective. Johnson & Johnson, Moderna, Novavax, Oxford AstraZeneca, Pfizer, Sinopharm, Sinovac, and Sputnik V, among others, are achieving good results. On the other hand, more than half of the world's population has been exposed to the virus. This has led to the appearance of more contagious strains, for example, in the United Kingdom, South Africa, and Brazil, among others. Many countries have already had several waves of COVID-19, and new ones are imminent. The herd-immunity threshold seems to be increasingly out of reach, and the world has still not entered a "post-pandemic" stage two years later.

The aim of this final chapter is not to forecast an unpredictable future, but, on the contrary, to examine the ethical-moral and sociopolitical challenges brought by the pandemic to our societies. Although my examples are taken mainly from Argentina, these can be extrapolated to most of the Western world if we bear in mind the specific characteristics of each country.

I will divide this topic into three different parts. The first part will address the ethical-moral dilemmas with which the pandemic has confronted us and our possible responses to them. The second part will deal with sociopolitical dilemmas. Here I will distinguish between global issues and problems that specifically affect Argentina. The third part will revisit Chapter 1 and the main theme of this book by relating these dilemmas to the dispute over representations of reality. It is here that the majority of ethical-moral and sociopolitical confrontations have taken place and will continue to do so. The level of representations accounts for sociological processes prior to and beyond the pandemic in that it accounts for contemporary "modes of subjectivation," to use Foucault's term.[2] In other words, it explains how the self (the "subject") is constructed by social discourses.

This analysis is based on a critical realist approach. It starts from the assumption that we can understand observable events only if we understand the unobservable structures that give rise to them. It is also based on the conviction that those sectors most interested in social welfare, equal rights, and even the very survival of the species have suffered a partial defeat in much of the Western world as a result of the abandoning of the precautionary principle in favor of "business as usual, whatever the cost." This is despite initial manifestations of care and solidarity that led thinkers as different as Slavoj Žižek or Naomi Klein to speak of the pandemic as an opportunity to transform capitalism.[3]

If truth be told, most Western societies abandoned the precautionary principle long before the pandemic began. Otherwise they would not have behaved as they did when faced with a catastrophe of such proportions. What I have tried to suggest in this book is that an effective response to the COVID-19 crisis (and other catastrophes) does not depend on quantitative factors (how many deaths are needed to shake us from our complacency) but qualitative ones (how to make the dead visible so that we can include them in our thought patterns and representations of reality).

This book is not a refuge for skeptics, pessimists, and other malcontents. On the contrary, I believe that recognizing these partial – but reversible – defeats can bring fresh life to the debate over social representations. Hopefully, the colossal health, social, political, and economic consequences of the pandemic will yield some insights into our selfish consumerist individualism which drives us to constantly play the victim, always clamoring for more rights. This will be the crucial step in deconstructing representations built on denial and paranoia.

For this reason, I also believe we should stop using metaphors like "the war on COVID-19." Viruses have neither consciousness nor any manifest intention to harm the human race. The real battle is not against the virus but over how to interpret our experience of the pandemic. The outcome will determine which actions are seen as feasible and desirable by the majority of society.

The debate is centered on two opposing worldviews. On the one hand, we have an ethic of mutual care, where people see themselves as members of a community. On the other, we have the *laissez faire* approach of the free market, where everyone is left to their own devices. Here, the winners are individuals in good health, with private medical care and legal or illegal access to vaccines. They live in spacious homes in which they can self-isolate if necessary and continue to work during lockdown. The losers are everybody else.

Ethical and moral dilemmas

In the first half of 2020, Daniel Loewe, a Chilean political and moral philosopher, published *Ethics and Coronavirus*. The book addresses several crucial questions regarding the dilemmas arising during the pandemic but which also predate it and go beyond it.[4] Interestingly, a central theme of the book is how social behavior is legitimized and how it can be transformed.

The precautionary principle and the debate between utilitarianism and deontology

The precautionary principle is important in ethical terms because it applies in situations with a high level of uncertainty. Decision-makers are forced to take a probabilistic approach that allows for errors (in particular, errors in calculating possible harm) and the consequences these could entail. Loewe defines this approach graphically by citing Cromwell's famous challenge to the General Assembly of the Church of Scotland shortly before the Battle of Dunbar – "I beseech you, in the bowels of Christ, think it possible you might be mistaken."

This phrase is particularly apt in the context of the pandemic, given repeated assurances from so-called "specialists" – in particular, liberal economists – that everything is under control. Among other falsehoods, they first assured us that the coronavirus was a sort of flu. Then, "herd immunity" was just around the corner. "Flattening the curve" and "mitigating" the circulation of the virus would be enough to prevent large numbers of deaths. Later, we were told that reopening schools would not spread the disease. These assurances have caused havoc in the Western world, with hundreds of thousands of deaths from COVID-19, as well as millions of other deaths from related causes. Meanwhile, the so-called experts have constantly evaded the precautionary principle, which requires us to act on the worst-case scenario.

Faced with an unquantifiable risk like the COVID-19 virus, Loewe argues that we should assume our first impressions are probably wrong. This being so, we need to review our options and ask ourselves what could happen in each case if our predictions fail. In situations of high uncertainty, the precautionary principle assumes that *every* course of action could be wrong and so chooses that of least harm.

Having established the primacy of the precautionary principle, Loewe devotes the rest of his book to exploring the ethical-moral issues related to the pandemic from both a utilitarian and a deontological viewpoint in order to determine the extent to which different interventions can be justified. In other words, he sets out to examine the ethical limits of the precautionary principle and how to choose between different types of harm: the harm that implementing the precautionary principle may cause and the harm it seeks to prevent.

The debate that Loewe establishes between utilitarianism and deontology aims to discover how best to legitimize our behavior. Utilitarianism argues that an action is right if it results in the happiness of the greatest number of people in a society or a group. Deontology, in contrast, takes a rule-based approach. Well-known examples of deontology are the Ten Commandments and the Universal Declaration of Human Rights. A utilitarian approach to the pandemic looks to see whether the harm caused by applying a specific public health measure is less than that caused by not applying it. But because everyone's happiness counts equally, a utilitarian approach has to juggle different types of harm, such as loss of life, reduction of life expectancy, loss of earnings, restriction of civil liberties, and loss of quality of life, among others. A deontological approach, on the other hand, places the protection of life and health above any other consideration. The duty of care is absolute since human dignity is not comparable or interchangeable with any other value or good, as it is in utilitarian calculations.

Both approaches are useful for explaining decision-making during the pandemic. Moreover – despite Loewe's predictions – they do not yield very different conclusions about the *consequences* of the decisions taken by various governments throughout 2020 and 2021. Of course, this information was not available to Loewe when he published the provocative questions in his book.

From a utilitarian point of view, it is now possible to confirm the validity of the lessons learned from the Spanish flu pandemic a century ago. Prioritizing other considerations over the precautionary principle during a pandemic of this magnitude (for example, the continued functioning of the economy as a whole or the importance of social gatherings and school attendance) ends up having a more damaging effect than suspending these temporarily. Countries that managed to stop the virus circulating by introducing a strict lockdown were able to return to normal in a matter of months. In contrast, countries that prioritized economic activities, face-to-face schooling, and social events (as happened with minor differences in most Western nations) continue to face high death and infection rates. Their economies also continue to suffer and show no signs of improvement as mutations of the virus begin to complicate vaccination policies.

From a deontological point of view, the conclusion is more straightforward and requires less verification. People's lives are more important than the economy or whether the rich have to pay a wealth tax to help tackle the social consequences of the pandemic. People's lives are more important than having to go without classroom education and social gatherings. The right to life is an absolute: all other rights can be sacrificed, if need be, to protect the lives of tens of thousands of people in a situation of uncertainty.

Nevertheless, although the two philosophical approaches used by Loewe to analyze the ethical-moral dilemmas of the pandemic yield similar conclusions, these conclusions are not shared by most citizens in the Western world. To understand this discrepancy, we need to look at other factors that predate the COVID-19 crisis. These have outweighed ethical-moral considerations and reflect both a different idea of community and a new contemporary subjectivity or vision of the world.

Questioning the precautionary principle

This section will deal with the criticisms of the protective measures which were considered necessary to deal with the pandemic in early 2020 but which were later abandoned if not directly ignored from the outset.

The first criticism was of a utilitarian nature, and Loewe devotes ample space to it in his book, as it shaped the agenda worldwide between March and July 2020. Put briefly, it claimed that lockdown policies overestimated the possible risks and would do more harm than good. However, the arguments supporting this claim were weak. In general, they have been disproved by events and, above all, by the obvious differences between societies that implemented restrictive measures and those that allowed the virus to circulate. It is worth reviewing some of these arguments in order to recall how seductive they sounded at the time.

1) *"Very few people will die from COVID-19 and this number does not justify so much effort and suffering on the part of the population as a whole."* In reality, between one and five people in a thousand have died of COVID-19 in most of the countries that allowed the virus to circulate freely.

2) *"The consequences of COVID-19 will be similar to those of a seasonal flu."* In fact, a year into the pandemic it was found that COVID-19 is between three and five times more lethal than influenza. In addition, it leaves important cardiological, respiratory, and neurological sequelae that have not been detected in other respiratory diseases. The outcome of these is still unknown.

3) *"Herd immunity can be obtained with a small number of infections."* Between April and June 2020, some scientists and public officials speculated that between 10 and 20 percent of infections in the general population would be enough to protect the population as a whole. As the first wave of the pandemic receded in some countries, they began looking for indicators to confirm these estimates. However, a second wave began in early 2021 in cities such as Manaus (Brazil), where about 75 percent of the population was thought to have been infected in the first wave in 2020. This wave produced more deaths than the previous one, so much so that hospitals ran short of oxygen. The massive reinfection rate showed that the immunity of a large part of the population has not lasted more than a few months, even when the herd-immunity threshold of 60–70 percent had been amply achieved.

4) *"The virus only affects the elderly."* It is true that people under 65 years of age in the developed world are 16–100 times less likely to die of COVID-19 than older people.[5] But the excess mortality in Argentina in 2020 – i.e. the number of deaths above and beyond what we would expect to see under normal conditions – reveals a worrying trend. It is men between 40 and 59 years of age that have shown the greatest difference in terms of life expectancy, with a loss of approximately 1.5 years in relation to previous years. This is without taking into account the appearance of important sequelae in all age groups. The long-term evolution of these sequelae and their possible impact on the life expectancy of young and adult populations of both sexes is unknown.

5) *"Mutations will make the virus less lethal."* These claims began to circulate toward the end of 2020, with the appearance of the first mutations. However, the most widely reported variants have proved to be equally deadly and contagious or even more so, with the exception of the Omicron variant, which is unclear at the moment of writing.

6) *"The economic and social effects of lockdown will be more destructive than the virus itself."* On the contrary, countries that applied severe restrictions recovered economically during the second half of 2020 and started 2021 with positive expectations. In contrast, prolonged uncertainty and the persistence of the disease have caused more social and psychological damage in societies that chose to prioritize the economy, face-to-face schooling, and social events. Successive waves of

infection and the repeated collapse of the health systems in these countries have left health workers, officials, and ordinary citizens exhausted and confused.

Supposedly utilitarian approaches to the pandemic based on the notion that "everyone's happiness counts equally" were soon outstripped by events. Nevertheless, none of the countries that relaxed the precautionary principle decided to return to it with the exception, perhaps, of Australia. On the contrary, restrictions have increasingly been relaxed with a consequent increase in the numbers of infections. Governments of developed countries are betting on resolving the crisis through mass vaccination.

A different challenge to the precautionary principle is the claim that the rules needed to ensure that precautions are complied with are "unfeasible" in this day and age for social and political reasons. Surprisingly, this argument does not originate among those who would have serious difficulty in complying with specific obligations for structural reasons – for example, lack of economic resources, crowded workspaces, and overcrowded living conditions. It comes from those whose problems (such as boredom and anguish) and needs (such as recreation, experimentation, and the search for the self) are much less about survival.

Now, the problems and needs of the affluent are something that many people in the world can only dream of. In Argentina, demonstrations against lockdown were not held by marginal unemployed workers or low income unionized workers, but by self-employed traders and professionals, and people from the better-off classes of society. The question of arguments which might legitimately be invoked by the underprivileged but which are in fact proposed by the affluent has been little explored in sociological studies on positioning with respect to the pandemic.

What is undeniable is that some cities, provinces, and even countries in the Western world managed to suppress the virus almost completely – at least for a while. The "unfeasibility" and "unsustainability" of strict public health measures is, therefore, speculation. Moreover, such arguments have been disproved by opinion polls. In Argentina, various polls have shown large numbers of people demanding *greater* restrictions from the state, despite a mood generated by the media that seems to suggest the contrary.[6]

Finally, the precautionary principle has also been challenged by some conservatives who assume that cooperation goes against human nature. Human beings, they argue, are selfish and guided only by self-interest. This notion throws an interesting light on the type of community in which we live. Although compatible with the notion of an all-pervasive culture of consumerism, it sees human nature as something static and immutable, part of the natural order rather than a state to be transformed.

However, the immutability of human nature is soon disproved by mobility analyses (studies that monitor travel and physical distancing) and the infection curves of the COVID-19 pandemic, which show that societies have behaved in every way possible. Some sectors of the population have never been careful; others have taken care all along; yet others have done so intermittently. This finding is confirmed by the opinion polls cited earlier. There is no binary division, then, between two clear-cut groups of people, no immutable behavior that would demonstrate the unalterable nature of our contemporary worldview – much less some fixed biological tendency. There are degrees of care, and most of the population moves up and down the continuum.

It will be remembered from Chapter 1 that a reproduction number (Rt) of more than 1.0 means the infection is spreading rapidly, while an Rt of less than 1.0 means it is not spreading and will eventually die out. Now, in Argentina and many other countries the Rt remained around 1.0 for several months. Only a little more care was needed to achieve an Rt below 1.0. So, the question is: which discourses and policies helped spread the virus and which hindered it? A general answer to this question is not enough: we need to look at the concrete consequences of each political, academic, or media communication. However, one thing is clear. Making excuses for carelessness has proved to be the surest way to undermine support for the restrictions protecting the public from COVID-19. On the other hand, recognizing and valuing those who take *more* care could have a positive impact. Surprisingly, this approach has hardly been attempted as a part of official policy in most Western countries, with interesting exceptions such as Australia, New Zealand, Norway, and Finland.

This is just one example of how moral and ethical dilemmas are related to social and political ones. It shows the need to abandon two overly simplistic views. The first is that contemporary subjectivity is something fixed and unchanging – a part of "human nature" – rather than the result of internalizing a consumerist and individualist culture. The second is that social behaviors can be understood in isolation. This book challenges both these assertions by attempting to show the interconnectedness of psychological mechanisms (denial, projection, paranoia, etc.), social behavior, and social and political responses to the pandemic.

In summary, we have seen that a utilitarian analysis demonstrates the comparative advantage of applying the precautionary principle during the pandemic and so bears out the deontological approach (which, of course, requires no empirical demonstration). This utilitarian analysis is a "natural experiment" that shows how infection and mortality rates (the dependent variable) have varied with different public health measures (the independent variable). Such a study includes whole populations, has a high ecological validity, and an almost nil chance of demand characteristics being present. The main confounding variable – incomplete reporting of cases – tends to disappear over time.

The question that arises, then, is why the precautionary principle was defeated in more than half of the planet. The answer to this question is no longer only philosophical in nature but requires some reflection on the way in which the social and political debates have been conducted in terms of both content and context. However, before moving on to this analysis, it is worth examining the shifting balance between current social perceptions of rights and responsibilities. Here, we are already at the boundary between philosophy, sociology, and politics.

Social perceptions of rights and responsibilities

Zygmunt Bauman uses the term "liquid modernity" to contrast the solid structures of classical modernity with the changing and uncertain period of late modernity or postmodernity.[7] As explained in the previous chapter, the breakdown of society in most developed Western countries has had to do with the destruction of responsibility as the guiding light of human behavior and a widespread notion of the individual as a mere "repository of rights." Paradoxically, this last notion has evolved out of the discourse on human rights.

"Solid" or classical modernity was based on a complex and dynamic balance between rights and obligations and on a culture that defined identity in terms of involvement in the processes of production. Individuals thought of themselves as "producers" – carpenters, merchants, doctors, architects, factory workers, bankers, clerks, etc. – and their identity was built on the basis of their own activities within the context of collective production.

Political theories in the social contract tradition, whether conservative, reformist, or revolutionary, were based on a balance between the rights and obligations arising from this productive role. Liberal thinkers such as Locke, Montesquieu, Rousseau, Kant, or Durkheim, who represented the bourgeois ideals of their time, and also Marx, Lenin, and Gramsci, among others who challenged them, all sought a balance between the rights and obligations of the different actors in the production matrix. As late as the 1960s, it was still assumed that subjects derived their identity from their role as producers and were responsible for their actions. This was one of the few points of agreement between Raymond Aron and Jean-Paul Sartre in their famous intellectual duel in *Le Monde*, where the two men argued on almost every topic, trivial or profound.

The debate between conservatives and reformists or revolutionaries (and the debates within these groups) was about the status quo. Conservative ideologies sought to defend it, and reformist and revolutionaries sought to improve it or reform it completely. In more complex cases, authors such as Max Weber, Norbert Elias, and even Pierre Bourdieu have shown a continuum between what was to be preserved and what was to be changed, with priorities changing over time. Nevertheless, the focus on rights and obligations was always the same.

The shift away from the focus on rights and obligations coincides with the rise of neoliberalism. Although rooted in modern liberalism (in particular, the ideas of John Stuart Mill, one of the fathers of utilitarianism), neoliberalism represents a more radical break with the past. It rejects all regulatory systems and limitations on "freedom" as inherently "inefficient" and "ineffective." Instead, it advocates "spontaneous," market-led developments and the commodification of all areas of human life. The new role of the subject as consumer was not yet clear to John Stuart Mill or his 19th-century contemporaries, who were still focused on the subject as producer. However, it can already be observed in some of the theories of the Chicago School, and in other 20th- century authors, such as Friedrich von Hayek, Ayn Rand, and Milton Friedman.

Neoliberalism extolls freedom as the supreme value, but it is different from the freedom aspired to in the 19th century. Freedom is no longer conceived in terms of being responsible for one's own destiny but merely as the ability to consume. This sort of freedom is available only to those who can afford it. It is no longer a universal value (an idea still present even in Stuart Mill) but only a value to be respected and demanded if one has accumulated enough wealth. And, as Marx pointed out, the "original accumulation of capital" is based on the extermination or oppression of others.

The 20th century is often described as a time of totalitarian regimes and an excess of state authority and state regulation. In reaction to this, contemporary subjects experience themselves as repositories of rights but no longer of obligations. They are consumers – but no longer producers – of social reality.

Bauman reflects in greater depth on these forms of "consumer style" subjectivity in works like *Community* and *Work, Consumerism and the New Poor*.[8] Social actors are no longer producers responsible for their actions. They are disengaged critics, disappointed with the products they are offered, and searching the market for new and better life styles, experiences, and ideals. Political parties and candidates exist to make these possible. Bauman likens this way of life to living on a camping site where "fleeting forms of association are more useful to people than long-term connections."[9] The inhabitants of today's world are like nomads with no ties to any community: they behave like alienated outsiders wherever they go.

Consumerist individuals can imagine no interest other than their own and are unable to imagine a "common interest" that is not related to business. Sadly, in questioning traditional assumptions about certainty, truth, and identity, deconstructionism has partly contributed to this new subjectivity by overemphasizing the importance of relativism, both at the epistemological and moral levels. This relativism goes to the extreme of denying even the possibility of a "common good" or "general interest." These are seen merely as imaginary constructs with no objective existence.

Deconstructionists believe it is only possible to analyze discourse as is used to legitimate different types of oppression. In this way, they have contributed to the vision of a society controlled by corporate interests, where any organized resistance or rebellion against oppression is simply a utopian dream. Perry Anderson offers a brilliant critique of the deconstructionist "cultural" left that, paradoxically, has alienated itself from the oppressed. At the same time, it has found new audiences by appealing to the subjectivity of the affluent sectors of the population.

This consumerist perspective compares what each political candidate, policy, or ideology has to "offer" (as if they were market products) and evaluates social action in terms of short-term self-interest rather than long-term collective interest. It thus constructs citizens as "clients" or "customers." Moreover, these citizens position themselves subjectively as victims. In doing so, they lose all sense of shame, guilt, or responsibility, as we saw in the previous chapter.

This new form of subjectivity is found at all social levels from the macropolitical to the family level. Parents, for example, increasingly seek their children's approval, behaving as "peers" rather than accepting the uncomfortable role of having to set limits, which has become a kind of taboo. Parents are afraid to openly say no to their children. If they discipline them at all, they do so in an impersonal way. The inability of parents to exert their authority is behind many of the psychological disorders suffered by children, adolescents, and young people today. These disorders are difficult to treat without understanding the changes in our subjective world that have taken place over the last two or three decades.

In the same way, the roles of teachers and other traditional figures of authority have been seriously undermined, especially in community settings. Even politicians and judges have been affected. Practices such as *lawfare* (which in Latin America used to mean criminalizing political protest but nowadays increasing refers to using the legal system to harm political opponents) are another sign of this difficulty in accepting rules. To confuse matters still further, corrupt politicians pretend to be victims of *lawfare*, too – with the full support of their respective political parties. Now, when justice is perceived to be arbitrary or, conversely, when politicians are seen to place themselves above the law, this corrodes the institutions, and society falls into a state of anomie, or social disorder. Conflicts are then increasingly solved through violence, where the cruelest and the most powerful tend to prevail – those who have the fewest inhibitions or external restrictions in exercising domination over others.

The unspoken pact against all types of authority includes both extreme liberals and a very significant sector of left-wing cultural critics who believe they are still fighting 20th-century authoritarianism by helping to undermine respect for any type of authority or institutions. In line with changes in social subjectivity, politicians nowadays seek to be liked rather than feared or respected as in the past. They will contradict themselves and make promises they cannot keep if this wins them the approval of the focus groups that consume much of the budget of contemporary political parties.

It is clear that this current crisis of authority does not apply to the marginal areas of poorer countries, where high levels of state repression are needed to prevent claims or needs from surfacing. But repression can also remain invisible. In many countries where voting is optional, the poor are voting less and less; consequently, they are excluded from political life. In other countries, they are seduced by various forms of fascism that allow them to project their hatred and resentment outside of the political system. The targets are usually immigrants from neighboring countries and even from other continents (e.g. Jews, Gypsies, and Arabs, among others). In some countries, the poor are seen as a threat that must be opposed by the organizations of "upstanding citizens." Here, repression is legitimized by stigmatizing the poor as "parasites" that lack the rights of "real" citizens – "people like you and me." Spanish philosopher Adela Cortina has coined the term *aporophobia* – literally, fear of poverty and poor people – to draw attention to this demonizing and dehumanizing of the poor.

If the poor are repressed in one way or another, the state has effectively given up on regulating the economic behavior of the wealthy thanks to the new social subjectivity mentioned earlier. This relinquishing of functions can be seen when governments reject progressive taxation in favor of a flat tax (or lower taxes for the wealthy) or when they refuse to intervene in the market to control price-setting mechanisms or regulate the financial sector. But it is also found at a more basic level in the way that the wealthy are allowed to get away with nearly everything from speeding and running stop signs to illegal property developments. The latter often take place in green zones, on public land, or on historical sites, with building codes being modified to legalize them retrospectively.

During the pandemic, it proved extremely difficult to make the well-to-do classes comply with public health regulations. Interestingly, lockdown restrictions rejected by Argentine travelers returning from abroad and the over 70s in middle-class neighborhoods of Buenos Aires were implemented without discussion in poor neighborhoods such as Villa Azul – and with excellent results. When such policies were more widely implemented in the province of Formosa in northeastern Argentina, they were quickly denounced as "human rights violations" although nothing of the kind seems to have occurred until March 2021, when the police of Formosa clamped down violently on a public demonstration.

Since ancient times, every society has been built on norms, whether codified or not. Every society, political party, neighborhood organization, club, or even group of friends needs to establish what is allowed and what is forbidden, what is advisable to maintain the social bond, and what is inadvisable. Groups may punish unacceptable behavior formally or informally. Informal sanctions include disapproving, criticizing, shaming, and even ostracism. Formal sanctions require exercising authority and – depending on the type of organization, may involve fines, suspension of membership, expulsion, etc. Even criminal organizations create their own codes of conduct and enforce them through different forms of punishment. These tend to be extremely harsh precisely because a bureaucracy is lacking to make them more nuanced.

Being part of a community is not only about receiving; it is also about giving. This implies developing certain behaviors as well as avoiding others. Not only clear rules but also clear sanctions are required for those who deviate. In some cases, we will participate in drawing up the rules but in most cases the rules will already exist. Unfortunately, one of the problems of contemporary individuals is their rejection of any sort of tradition or inherited values. Thus, they tend to treat any norm they have not helped to create themselves as something foreign and unacceptable. This gives rise to a growing anomie within the group and within society as a whole.

Now, many rules become obsolete and need to be changed after a time. Some rules promote democratic participation and egalitarian policies, but others are profoundly undemocratic and even oppressive. However, no group of any size can function without rules and established procedures, without authorities in charge of enforcing them, and without consequences for those who violate them. Unfortunately, anyone who points this out nowadays risks being branded as "moralistic" and "authoritarian." The illusion prevails that norms require everybody's agreement or that we have the right to "negotiate" our level of compliance, whatever the norm or the justification for its existence. In the context of a pandemic, this is a threat to the very survival of the species.

It is true that obsolete or repressive norms have been collectively confronted at different moments in history. But this has usually been done by individuals promoting alternative systems of norms intended to improve the common good – or at least to benefit historically persecuted or excluded groups. In general, enforcing social change through reform or revolution has required even *greater* authority since change is always resisted by those who enjoyed power and privileges during the previous era. Imposing a new norm requires much greater authority than upholding one already sanctioned by centuries-old or millenary tradition. The truth is that every successful reformist or revolutionary movement has understood this, from the Radicals of 19th-century Britain, who created government inspectors to enforce reforms, to the Chinese Communist Party, which introduced electronic surveillance of all its citizens in 2020 to enforce behaviors considered desirable by the state. Only the cultural left in the West has forgotten that strong authority and organization is needed to overcome resistance to change.

In this sense, it is essential to distinguish between a revolutionary who seeks to transform society and an individual who wants to drop out of the social contract. Nowadays, both are called "rebels." However, regardless of our own idea of social justice, the revolutionary is legitimized because he or she seeks to replace an unjust order with a more just one. In contrast, neoliberal "rebellion" seeks to eliminate all forms of regulation, whether the arguments come from the left or from the right. In turn, this new form of subjectivity is subordinated to an "adolescentization" of identity, which supports what has already been said about forms of infantilization. This profound refocusing of the ethical and moral debate seems not to have registered sufficiently at the political level to make coordinated and effective action possible in crises such as the pandemic.

In the 20th century, the conservative right defended the interests of the dominant classes, the socialist left fought to empower the working classes, while the liberal center defended the middle classes – at least in theory.[10] In the 21st century, these assumptions need a radical overhaul. Our new social subjectivity threatens the legitimacy of any system of values. This issue is fundamental and needs to be resolved before we can even begin a political debate from whatever ideological position we may hold.

To end this section, I would like to return to two important points. At the individual level, Luigi Zoja points out the importance of the individual conscience for resisting the morally deadening effect of consumerism:

> A major challenge in the coming years, therefore, will be that of maintaining, amid the indifference of the masses and the anaesthesia of consumerism, a capacity for indignation. This should have two directions: an impulse towards rectifying wrongs committed by others, but at the same time shame for our own transgressions. Ultimately, the mobilization of credible moral feelings arises in the solitude of the individual

conscience; and it mistrusts crusades aimed at the masses, propagated by media multipliers.[11]

At the social level, the main challenge is to reconstruct a sense of community that will allow us to think once again in terms of collective welfare. The abstract notion of freedom proclaimed by neoliberalism as a guide to social action must be counterbalanced by notions of equality, impartiality, and fairness. Rules and norms are needed to impose limits on the powerful through collective and solidary action.

Sociopolitical dilemmas

From both a utilitarian and a deontological perspective, a comparison of different public policies for managing the pandemic clearly confirms the advantages of implementing the precautionary principle. An analysis of the ways in which rights and obligations are generally perceived in our modern consumerist society and contemporary forms of social subjectivity allows us to understand some of the obstacles encountered in implementing this principle.

Ultimately, these disputes must be settled at the sociopolitical level. Here it is crucial to ask ourselves about the role of systems of representation as determinants of action. It is with this in mind that I will end this book by returning to the topic of representations with which it began.

How can we make a sociopolitical assessment of the COVID-19 pandemic? Arguably, the pandemic has exposed our inability to challenge the dominant vision of reality and to implement cooperative measures during a catastrophe. The effects of this vision have been demoralizing in terms of both morality and morale. In this sense, most Western societies have viewed the pandemic in the same way as the global climate crisis: the level of death and destruction was not enough to justify across-the-board restrictions, even when health systems were collapsing. The most striking evidence was denied or ignored in the hope of being able to continue life as usual – even if this led to the extinction of the human race. The doubt that remains is to what extent governments acted – or failed to act – because of pressure or approval from the wider population.

The breakdown of society in many Western countries has been a gradual and recursive process. If this process is to be reversed, an honest appraisal is required – one that accounts for two partial but interrelated phenomena: the sacrificing of public health and safety for the sake of corporate profits; and the declining role of the state as a guarantor of public interests. Although these phenomena have not occurred equally throughout the planet and are by no means complete, fixed states, they undoubtedly account for the main political developments in much of the West. And, within this universe, Argentina has characteristics of its own that are also worth examining.

The defeat of the precautionary principle

When we decide to take precautions against an unknown virus, we do so to avoid infecting others as much as ourselves. We accept responsibility for our actions and we choose cooperation over mere selfishness. However, this is not only an altruistic commitment, it also involves reciprocity. We do something for others in the hope that they will do the same for us. That is the win-win situation. In the case of a pandemic, we find strength and encouragement from observing the positive results of public health measures in our society. Other natural and social disasters that may appear during our lifetime can be overcome in a similar way.

As I have already mentioned, the precautionary principle is recommended in situations with high levels of uncertainty. Prevention-focused decisions assume a worst-case scenario, precisely because the hazards are unknown and the stakes are high. They necessarily err on the side of caution. The precautionary principle replaces the unpredictable outcomes of allowing the virus to circulate for other more foreseeable outcomes, such as the redistribution of income necessary to cushion the economic and social impact of lockdown. As we have seen, this option was clearly the best, both from a deontological point of view and from the point of view of the most straightforward economic utilitarianism. In February and March 2020, there was no reliable information about the contagiousness and lethality of the virus, its mutations, or possible sequelae. Some of these variables are now better understood, but others remain undetermined.

Unfortunately, however, Argentina's initial commitment to the precautionary principle and to the value of life over immediate economic interests soon ran out of steam. In March 2020, the country's policies seemed closer to those of East Asia, Australasia, and some Scandinavian countries. Nevertheless, they quickly mutated into a set of contradictory measures with results similar to the infection curve of Sweden, which had opted – disastrously – for herd immunity. Unfortunately, Argentina's structural problems are much worse than Sweden's in terms of its health system, economic organization, social relations, GDP, and income distribution.

Another difference between Sweden and Argentina is that the Argentine government never made the change of strategy explicit, while Sweden made its preference for herd immunity clear from the outset. Instead, the Argentine government maintained a discourse based on the precautionary principle and the priority of health over all other considerations, which was consistent neither with the health and political measures deployed nor the results obtained.

From a promising beginning in March 2020, the Argentine government gradually became increasingly entangled in its own contradictions. In May 2020, the virus began to spread throughout the Metropolitan Area of Buenos Aires. At the same time, the government began to lift restrictions on commercial activities in a sort of schizophrenia. All this was accompanied by a series of presidential *faux-pas*, including birthday parties with friends and a barbecue with union leaders – without social distancing or face masks – when social gatherings were expressly forbidden. Meanwhile, the government made increasingly abstract appeals for individual responsibility, bringing the social bond closer to neoliberal subjectivities than the initial commitment to a "state and collective responsibility" based on the precautionary principle.

This growing contradiction in Argentina between official declarations and the policies actually implemented seriously undermined the government's authority. Supporters of "openness" and "freedom" continued to criticize the discourse of care and restrictions and the so-called "eternal quarantine" in the Buenos Aires region. In particular, they criticized the president, who appeared to be reluctant to remove restrictions. He finally did remove them, mainly because of pressure from the government of the Autonomous City of Buenos Aires. A growing number of public demonstrations against lockdown were held by vociferous minorities. These protests, although small, attracted a lot of media attention because they were either discouraged or directly prohibited, depending on where they were held. Prohibitions were not enforced, however, due to a lack of will and resources, and also because governments in Argentina only use the security forces against poor people. Fines and sanctions against those who violated lockdown restrictions were insignificant, and administrative proceedings were usually dismissed.

At the same time, the Argentine government also paid the health, economic, and political costs of a massive circulation of the virus, both in terms of infections and deaths and the risk of new strains and variants. It partly lost the support of its most loyal voters, who were convinced of the importance of health measures and strengthening the authority of the state. All this was accompanied by a constant inability on the part of the national health authorities to understand the importance of testing, contact tracing, and isolation mechanisms as a way of containing the spread of the virus. The strategy of "flattening the curve" to prevent the health system collapsing (instead of suppressing community transmission of the virus) was common to both national and provincial policies, with the notable exception of the province of Formosa.

Beyond the mistakes of the moment, the defeat of the precautionary principle has had much more worrying consequences. These include the discrediting of public health policies and the feeling that it will make no difference whether we obey COVID-19 regulations in future or not, just as it has made no difference until now whether we had a system of tracking and isolation of cases and close contacts.

The general perception of the pandemic in Argentina is now more or less as follows:

a) The "longest quarantine in the world" was useless.
b) Those who died would have died anyway.
c) Without the "quarantine" the economy would not have had any problems and would have recovered faster from the economic crisis that began during the previous government.
d) It is not possible to prevail against the interests of the most concentrated sectors of economic power.
e) In short, in this particular case, the COVID skeptics were right.

Some skeptics argued that those who violated the quarantine restrictions did society a favor by accelerating the arrival of the epidemic "peak" and so allowing restrictions to be lifted more quickly. This argument, absurd as it may sound, has many supporters – and not only among the more radical opposition groups. Indeed, it makes sense in the context of the general perception I have just outlined. At the root of this perception is the assumption that the pandemic would have spread anyway. In this view, the only things the government could have influenced were the timing of the epidemic peaks, the attempts to prevent the collapse of the health system, and the significant number of additional deaths for reasons not related to COVID-19.

These assumptions do not comport too well with the concrete observables and indicators available both globally and locally. But, as we have seen, observables require structures of assimilation – abstract conceptual schemes that can integrate them into a way of making sense of our life experiences. Thus, the situation in Argentina ended up becoming one of the worst on the planet in terms of the dispute over representations. The way in which the debate has been conducted and its general assumptions and conclusions have left little room for critical or counter-hegemonic views that could have any important political impact. This is quite unlike what has happened in countries with more explicitly negationist governments.

In countries such as the United States, Brazil, or Sweden, important currents have emerged to question the health decisions of their governments. They have made visible the consequences of abandoning the precautionary principle in the number of excess deaths or the better economic performance of countries that decided to suppress the virus before resuming activities. These countries include China, South Korea, Vietnam, Australia, and New Zealand, among others.

This issue is no small one. It explains to a large extent why Donald Trump, who seemed certain to be reelected before the pandemic, lost the United States presidential election in November 2020. The mishandling of the pandemic seems to have been the main reason for the fall of the Republican leader in many states that until then had supported him. In Brazil, the political effects of denial have been less obvious. But the results of the municipal elections at the end of 2020 were not particularly favorable to President Jair Bolsonaro. These results appeared before the catastrophic resurgence of COVID-19 in Manaus in January 2021 and before the confirmation of a new Brazilian strain of the virus – the Gamma variant. Presumably, these events will influence the debate during Brazil's next presidential elections in 2022. It also remains to be seen how Sweden's mismanagement of the pandemic (notorious in comparison with its neighbors) will affect the country's 2022 elections.

In contrast, Argentina, like Spain, has not managed to analyze the consequences of "openness." Both countries are caught in the denialism resulting from a political discourse that supports the precautionary principle and public policies that do the opposite. Instead, the negative consequences of the pandemic (economic, social, educational, and even health) are attributed to a failed public health policy. In fact, the policy was never properly applied.

Perhaps the most convincing evidence can be found in those cases where the precautionary principle was in fact applied successfully. In Argentina, this occurred in the province of Formosa, which suffered a very low rate of infections and deaths during 2020 that, projected at the national level, would have meant having saved between 40,000 and 45,000 people during the same year. In contrast, the promises made by the Argentine government at the end of December 2020 to vaccinate all high risk groups in February and March before the second wave proved to be illusory. By ignoring the problems of obtaining and distributing the necessary doses, the government once again created a contradiction between official statements and reality. Eventually, the government did manage to acquire a significant number of vaccine doses. This was no mean achievement in a market dominated by Europe, Japan, and the United States, but it paled in the face of exaggerated promises, such as those made in December 2020.

Something similar happened with other measures, such as the emergency family income (known as IFE), the aid to companies, and the freezing of rents. Despite their novelty and effectiveness, they too paled in comparison with excessive presidential promises to the effect that no one would be left to face the catastrophe single-handedly. This caused enormous unrest among the lower-middle and middle classes, who were especially hard hit during the first year of the pandemic.

The defeat of the precautionary principle is one of the most serious legacies of the pandemic. It encourages those sectors of society that favor individualism – as opposed to solidarity and cooperation – to continue their selfish behavior. What is significant, too, is not just that the precautionary principle was defeated but the way in which it was defeated. In Argentina, the truth was hidden behind a smoke screen of official speeches. This confused a large part of the population, who were unable to register what was happening, much less construct a version of events different from that presented in the media.

Unless we take stock of this partial defeat, we will soon reach a point of no return. Our response to a fifth or tenth wave of the pandemic or to any other catastrophic event will always start from this new bedrock of learning. Knowledge is constructed fundamentally through analogies with previous situations and extends the ways in which these are represented.

The defeat of the role of the state

The second level of defeat is related to the previous one, but its consequences are more far-reaching. It is the defeat of the state, not only as the implementer of public health care policies but also as the enforcer of legal norms.

In March and April 2020, the president of Argentina was still in his inaugural year. He had been elected with a high percentage of votes (48 percent) with the promise of state intervention to put Argentina back on its feet after two years of recession, high inflation, and growing unemployment and poverty. At that time, there was an obvious need for the country to face the threat of the pandemic as a community. It was clear that the "laws of the market" could not in any way replace this function.

Addressing the population in a pastoral role (a classic leadership role analyzed most revealingly by Michel Foucault), the Argentine president proposed to "lead" social action by defining norms and imposing limits.[12] Nevertheless, this pastorship in particular did not call for popular support or consolidation of the measures but for trust in the paternal (Rita Segato would say maternal) leadership of the presidential figure.[13] Perhaps one of the high points in this exercise of authority was the president's reaction to a decision to lay off almost 1,500 workers by Techint, an Italian-Argentinian engineering conglomerate. Alberto Fernandez declared on March 29: "Let me tell you right now that I will not let them do it." And he added, in a clear exercise of his authority as representative of the people and especially its most disadvantaged sectors: "Well, guys, it's your turn to earn less."

Not surprisingly, a saucepan-bashing "cacerolazo" protest was held the day after these statements, demanding a reduction in politician's salaries. Yet, a salary cut of 20 percent, such as that applied in Uruguay, could have been accompanied by a larger wealth tax, rather than capping the tax at 3.5 percent on wealth in Argentina and 5.25 percent on wealth outside the country as finally happened. The opportunity to nip anti-politics in the bud was lost. The "cacerolazo" broke the consensus generated by the president in his "pastoral" function and undermined the role of the state in managing the crisis.

The repeated U-turns in different political decisions and public health measures from that moment onward, beginning with the failed expropriation of the bankrupt soymeal exporter Vicentin, dented the president's authority. Now, when the state withdraws from providing reliable information, guiding public health measures, and punishing those who endanger the lives and health of others, the power to influence society shifts elsewhere. The careful begin to feel their efforts and sacrifices are in vain. Whatever they do, the virus continues to spread and people continue to die. And so the temptation to let things slide becomes stronger – especially when there is no authority and no penalties for offenders.

Thus, those who followed the rules from the beginning gradually lost the moral authority to question those who did not. Carelessness gradually became the norm, and those who are still convinced of the need for responsible attitudes feel isolated and powerless. Day by day, it becomes increasingly difficult to tell people to wear their face masks properly, to socially distance, to keep public spaces properly ventilated, and to apply other anti-coronavirus measures. On the contrary, such requests tend to be met with scorn or incredulity.

Thus, legitimacy has slowly shifted from the careful to the careless. The still large number of people who continue to respect the norms (to protect themselves, or others, or both) do so silently, almost ashamed, and apologizing for "going overboard." Representations and behaviors have become negotiable. Except for certain minority groups, most people are now more or less careful (or careless) depending on the people around them. They vary their actions from day to day based on the behavior and expectations of others.

Although it has become more prominent during the pandemic, the role of the state has been one of the most important political debates of the past 100 years and is contentious at the national, regional, and international levels.

Choosing how to tell this story

The mere existence of legislation does not guarantee compliance. Just as laws require enforcement, they also require social legitimation to establish their importance and necessity. This legitimation creates social sanctions for those who do not respect the laws and which are usually as or more effective than state sanctions. A very clear case is how smoking in enclosed public places has become negatively evaluated over time. A failed case is the attempt to improve compliance with traffic regulations in Argentina, which continues to have one of the highest death rates from road accidents in the world per head of population.

Antonio Gramsci is one of the most important authors who analyzed the ways in which social legitimation is construed. He suggested that

> the starting-point of critical elaboration is the consciousness of what one really is, and is "knowing thyself" as a product of the historical process to date which has deposited in you an infinity of traces, without leaving an inventory. Such an inventory must therefore be made at the outset.[14]

That "critical elaboration" means the ways in which we can tell our stories to ourselves. And that stories also involve ways of social legitimation.

The battle for meaning is fought on three interconnected levels: cognitive, emotional, and ethical-moral. There is a constant interplay between (1) the information we accept and the observables we are able to process; (2) the emotions that predominate at a particular moment; and (3) the model of community we support.

The need to fight the infodemic aggravated by false information, conspiracy theories, rumors, disinformation campaigns, etc. is very clear. But my perception is that today the dispute is not only or even fundamentally on that level but on the other two levels, which have been the main focus of this book.

On the emotional level, we can surrender to denialism and normalize that process, or we can respond to the pain of other people's suffering. We can surrender to weariness, boredom, or feelings of helplessness, or we can examine our behavior and make room for shame as a first step toward becoming better people. We can learn from our weaknesses, repair the damage done through carelessness, and to allow responsibility to emerge.

At the ethical-moral level, the pandemic has confronted us with these disputes that go back to the very origin of modern nation-states and the political struggles of the last century, including disputes over globalization. We find two conflicting ways of representing society, or rather the society we wish to belong to, each based on a different set of emotions. Nevertheless, our society includes an enormous majority of people who do not know, or who are undecided, or whose behavior is inconsistent. Ultimately, we are all driven by selfishness and solidarity. It is not possible to find the right moral balance between these two impulses at all times and places or in every situation.

The dispute over representations of the pandemic will not stop at the pandemic, nor will it affect only health issues. It is a litmus test for an infinite number of sociopolitical disputes, and, of course, it will also affect social representations of reality. In short, this battle is being played out – like any other conflict – in the minds and hearts of each of us. Only what is at stake here is the kind of world we want to live in. Accepting defeat is a necessary condition to reverse what has happened during this pandemic. It does not imply giving up, but, on the contrary, imagining that there are ways of life that do not imply surrendering to the law of the strongest and cruelest. The latter occurs when the "invisible hand" of the market becomes the final arbiter of our destiny.

To engage in a meaningful argument about representations of the pandemic, we need to recover values that were buried in much of the Western world after the first months of 2020. We must first make room for them in our imagination if we are to build a community that benefits everyone – a community that redistributes wealth more equitably and looks after the majority of its members. This has been the dream of many generations – a dream that now threatens to be stifled by the mantra of individualism ("you can only rely on yourself") and the notion that the "selfish gene" in us will always prevail.

Sigmund Freud defined responsibility in a very provocative way, and the Argentine psychoanalyst Silvia Bleichmar redefined it to confront ourselves against our challenges, dreams, and nightmares: "To take responsibility is to recognize that this strange thing that appears at night is something that belongs to me."[15]

Yes, those strange feelings that appear in the worst hours of this pandemic do *really* belong to us. But we can dream of confronting them differently, as part of a community of peers fighting for a fairer and more egalitarian world.

Notes

1 A systematic review of 57 studies comprising more than 250,000 survivors of COVID-19 has shown that over half of COVID-19 survivors experienced post-acute sequelae six months after recovery. See Destin Groff et al., "Short-Term and Long-Term Rates of Postacute Sequelae of SARS-CoV-2 Infection: A Systematic Review," *JAMA Network Open* 4, no. 10 (2021), October 13, 2021, https://jamanetwork.com/journals/jamanetworkopen/fullarticle/2784918.

2 According to Foucault, subjectivation is the process by which we acquire the subjectivity that allows us to shape our conduct and personality. In his later writings, Foucault argues that "subjectivation is a formative power of the self, surpassing the structures of knowledge and power from out of which it

emerges." Bindeshwar Prasad Mandal, *A Handbook of Sociology* (New Delhi: K.K. Publications, 2021), 166.

3 For Slavoj Žižek, see *Pandemic!: COVID-19 Shakes the World* (New York & London: OR Books, 2020), and *Pandemic! 2. Chronicles of a Lost Time* (New York: Polity Press, 2021). For Naomi Klein, see "A Message from the Future II: The Years of Repair," *The Intercept*, October 1, 2020, https://theintercept.com /2020/10/01/naomi-klein-message-from-future-covid/.

4 Daniel Loewe, *Ética y coronavirus* (Buenos Aires: Fondo de Cultura Económica, 2020).

5 John P. A. Ioannidis, Cathrine Axfors, and Despina G. Contopoulos-Ioannidis, "Population-Level COVID-19 Mortality Risk for Non-elderly Individuals Overall and for Non-elderly Individuals without Underlying Diseases in Pandemic Epicenters," *Environmental Research* 188 (2020), https://www.scien-cedirect.com/science/article/pii/S0013935120307854.

6 The work of the Institute of Economy and Society in Contemporary Argentina of the National University of Quilmes is particularly worth mentioning. The Institute carried out two very striking opinion surveys about the pandemic with large samples in the city and province of Buenos Aires in January and February 2021. The data reflects high support for the care measures, as well as consider-able attempts by significant sectors of the population to implement care norms in addition to those of the state. See Javier Balsa, Guillermo de Martinelli, Pehuén Romaní, and Juan I. Spólita, "¿Qué se debería haber hecho frente a la pandemia? La opinión de la ciudadanía," Agencia Paco Urondo, February 4, 2021, https:// www.agenciapacourondo.com.ar/debates/que-se-deberia-haber-hecho-frente-la -pandemia-la-opinion-de-la-ciudadania.

7 See Zygmunt Bauman, *Liquid Modernity* (Cambridge: Polity, 2000).

8 Zygmunt Bauman, *Work, Consumerism and the New Poor* (Buckingham: Open, 2005); and Zygmunt Bauman, *Community Seeking Safety in an Insecure World* (Cambridge: Polity, 2001).

9 Richard Sennett, *The Corrosion of Character: The Personal Consequences of Work in the New Capitalism* (New York: W. W. Norton & Co., 1998), 23, cited in Zygmunt Bauman, *Liquid Modernity, op. cit.*, 149.

10 Seymour Martin Lipset, *Political Man: The Social Bases of Politics* (Garden City, NY: Doubleday, 1960), 222, https://archive.org/details/politicalmansoc i00inlips.

11 Luigi Zoja, *Paranoia: The Madness that Makes History* (London and New York: Routledge, 2017), 282.

12 Michel Foucault, *Omnes et Singulatim: Towards a Criticism of 'Political Reason'*. The Tanner Lectures on Human Values. Delivered at Stanford University October 10 and 16, 1979. Available online at: https://www.academia .edu/34116882/Michel_Foucault_Omnes_et_Singulatim_Towards_a_Criticism _of_Political_Reason_The_Tanner_Lectures_on_Human_Values_delivered_at _Stanford_University_October_10_and_16_1979.

13 See, for example, the interview (in Spanish) conducted by Alejandro Bercovich in the program *Brotes Verdes*: https://www.youtube.com/watch?v=L5JjUAW82is.

14 Antonio Gramsci, "Notes for an Introduction and an Approach to the Study of Philosophy and the History of Culture," in *The Gramsci Reader. Selected Writings 1916–1935*, edited by David Forgacs (New York: New York University Press, 2000), 326.

15 Silvia Bleichmar, *Vergüenza, culpa y pudor* (Buenos Aires: Paidós, 2016), 518.

Bibliography

Agamben, Giorgio, *Where We Are Now. The Epidemic as Politics* (New York and London: Rowman and Littlefield, 2021).

Bachelard, Gaston, *The Formation of the Scientific Mind. A Contribution to the Psychoanalisis of Objective Knowledge* (Manchester: Clinamen, 2002 [1938]).

Balsa, Javier, "Strategies against the COVID-19 Pandemic and the Crisis of Hegemony," *Notebooks: The Journal for Studies on Power* 1, no. 1 (2021): 96–119, https://doi.org/10.1163/26667185-01010006.

Balsa, Javier, G. de Martinelli, P. Romaní, and J.I. Spólita, "¿Qué se debería haber hecho frente a la pandemia? La opinión de la ciudadanía," *Agencia Paco Urondo*, February 4, 2021, https://www.agenciapacourondo.com.ar/debates/que-se-deberia-haber-hecho-frente-la-pandemia-la-opinion-de-la-ciudadania.

Baudrillard, Jean, *The Consumer Society* (Paris: Gallimard, 1970 [1998]).

Bauman, Zygmunt, *Liquid Modernity* (Cambridge: Polity, 2000).

Bauman, Zygmunt, *Community. Seeking Safety in an Insecure World* (Cambridge: Polity, 2001).

Bauman, Zygmunt, *Work, Consumerism and the New Poor* (Berkshire and New York: Open University Press, 2005).

Beck, Ulrich, *Risk Society: Towards a New Modernity* (London and New York: Sage, 1992).

Berger, Peter and Thomas L. Luckmann, *The Social Construction of Reality. A Treatise in the Sociology of Knowledge* (New York: Doubleday, 1966).

Bleichmar, Silvia, *Vergüenza, culpa y pudor* (Buenos Aires, Paidós, 2016).

Cohen, Stanley, *States of Denial: Knowing about Atrocities and Suffering* (Cambridge, UK: Blackwell Publishers, 2001).

Dawkins, Richard, *The Selfish Gene* (Oxford: Oxford University Press, 1976).

Feierstein, Daniel, "Political Violence in Argentina and its Genocidal Characteristics," *Journal of Genocide Research* 8, no. 2 (2006): 149–168, https://doi.org/10.1080/14623520600703024.

Feierstein, Daniel, *Genocide as Social Practice. Reorganizing Society under Nazism and the Argentina Military Juntas* (New Jersey: Rutgers University Press, 2014).

Feierstein, Daniel, *La construcción del enano fascista. Los usos del odio como estrategia política en Argentina* (Buenos Aires: Capital Intelectual, 2020).

Foucault, Michel, *The History of Sexuality Volume 1: An Introduction* (London: Allen Lane, 1979 [1976]).

Foucault, Michel, *Omnes et Singulatim: Towards a Criticism of 'Political Reason'*. The Tanner Lectures on Human Values. Delivered at Stanford University October 10 and 16, 1979.

Freud, Sigmund, "Formulations on the Two Principles of Mental Functioning" (1911), in *The Standard Edition of the Complete Psychological Works of Sigmund Freud* (London: The Hogarth Press and the Institute of Psycho-Analisis), Volume XII, 1958.

Freud, Sigmund, "Beyond the Pleasure Principle" (1920), in *The Standard Edition of the Complete Psychological Works of Sigmund Freud* (London: The Hogarth Press and the Institute of Psycho-Analisis, 1955), Volume XVIII.

Gramsci, Antonio, "Notes for an Introduction and an Approach to the Study of Philosophy and the History of Culture," in *The Gramsci Reader. Selected Writings 1916–1935*, edited by David Forgacs (New York: New York University Press, 2000).

Groff, Destin, et al., "Short-Term and Long-Term Rates of Postacute Sequelae of SARS-CoV-2 Infection A Systematic Review," *JAMA Network Open* 4, no. 10 (2021), October 13, 2021. https://jamanetwork.com/journals/jamanetworkopen/fullarticle/2784918.

Ioannidis, John P.A., Cathrine Axfors, and Despina G. Contopoulos-Ioannidis, "Population-Level COVID-19 Mortality Risk for Non-Elderly Individuals Overall and for Non-Elderly Individuals without Underlying Diseases in Pandemic Epicenters," *Environmental Research* 188 (2020), https://www.sciencedirect.com/science/article/pii/S0013935120307854.

Klein, Naomi, "A Message from the Future II: The Years of Repair," *The Intercept*, October 1, 2020, https://theintercept.com/2020/10/01/naomi-klein-message-from-future-covid/.

Lipset, Seymour Martin, *Political Man: The Social Bases of Politics* (Garden City: Doubleday, 1960).

Loewe, Daniel, *Ética y Coronavirus* (Buenos Aires: Fondo de Cultura Económica, 2020).

Mandal, Bindeshwar Prasad, *A Handbook of Sociology* (New Delhi: K.K. Publications, 2021).

Puget, Janine and René Kaës (comp.), *Violencia de Estado y psicoanálisis* (Buenos Aires and México: Lumen, 2006).

Sennett, Richard, *The Corrosion of Character: The Personal Consequences of Work in the New Capitalism* (London and New York: W. W. Norton & Company, 1998).

Tangney, June Price and Ronda L. Dearing, *Shame and Guilt* (New York: The Guilford Press, 2002).

Žižek, Slavoj, *Pandemic!: COVID-19 Shakes the World* (New York & London: OR Books, 2020).

Žižek, Slavoj, *Pandemic! 2. Chronicles of a Lost Time* (New York: Polity Press, 2021).

Zoja, Luigi, *Paranoia: The Madness that Makes History* (London and New York: Routledge, 2017).

Index

Foucault, M. 69, 77, 95
Franco, F. 38
Freud, S. 17, 32–35, 56–57, 98
Friedman, M. 85
genocide 2, 6, 32, 34, 41, 58; Argentine
  genocide 33–34, 39, 43; Nazi
  genocide 42, 66

Giordano, V. 40
Gramsci, A. 5, 51, 87, 97
grand narratives 68
gratification 64; ability to postpone
  17, 28n17; delayed 17; inability to
  postpone 47
Grossman, H. 65–66
guilt, feelings of 5, 58, 67–72, 86

H1N1 influenza (2009) 1
"hammer and the dance, The" (Pueyo)
  20–21
Han, Byung-Chul 1
Heidegger, M. 12
herd immunity 15–16, 19, 49, 78,
  81, 91
human rights: organizations 22, 29n23,
  79; violations 43, 88

individualism 75, 95; faces of 50;
  hyper-individualism 67; irresponsible
  70; liberal 75; mantra of 98; selfish
  5, 77
individual projections 57, 58
individual psychopathologies 58
infectatorship 25, 51
*Initiative for the Protection of Human
  Rights COVID-19* 29n23
Inter-American Commission on Human
  Rights 43
isolation 34, 93; ASPI 22; ASPO 22;
  policies 15; social 40

Jayyusi, L. 11
Jewish resistance 66; groups 42; to
  Nazism 43
Jews: creating conspiracy about
  pandemic 60; instinct of self-
  preservation 65–67; perceptions of
  German and Polish 44; strategies of
  denial 41
Johnson & Johnson (vaccine) 76

Judenräte 65, 73n13
Just world thinking 44, 45

Kaczerginski, S. 66
Kaës, R. 37
Kant, I. 84
Klein, N. 77
Kofman, E. 16, 22

Lacordaire, J. B. (Dominican priest) 68
laissez faire approach 78
Language of Psychoanalysis
  (Laplanche and Pontalis) 56
Laplanche, J. 56–57
Latin America 26; Covid-19 pandemic
  in 18–20; herd strategy in 18–19;
  victims during pandemic in 40
Lemkin, R.6
Le Monde (Aron and Sartre) 84
Lenin, Vladimir 84
local grass-roots organizations 22
lockdown 15, 20–25, 40, 45–47, 59–60,
  62, 80, 82, 87, 92
Locke, John 84
Loewe, D. 78–80
López, M. P. 63–64

Marx, K. 11–12, 84
mathematical modeling, use of 16
Milanović, B. 17
Mill, J. S. 85
minimization 44–48
"mitigating" circulation of virus 78
mobility analyses 83
Moderna (vaccine) 76
modesty 69, 70
Montesquieu 84
moralizing 68; accusations of 63, 69;
  religions 68

narcissistic contract 37, 38
narratives 39, 46, 68
National Council for Scientific and
  Technical Research (CONICET)
  15–16, 22, 53n13
National University of Rosario 22
natural disasters 32
Nazis(m) 66; genocide 42, 66;
  occupation 67; propaganda 42;
  survivors 39

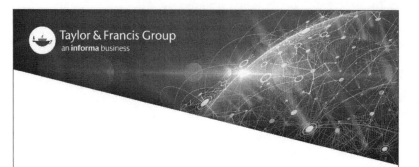

For Product Safety Concerns and Information please contact our EU
representative GPSR@taylorandfrancis.com Taylor & Francis Verlag GmbH,
Kaufingerstraße 24, 80331 München, Germany

Printed and bound by CPI Group (UK) Ltd, Croydon, CR0 4YY
11/04/2025
01844010-0006

"Daniel Feierstein's basic contention is controversial but convincing: despite its biological origin, the COVID-19 pandemic was primarily a social phenomenon. Politicians of all stripes failed to fully grasp that fact. Understanding state policies, civil responses, outcomes, and long-term consequences requires sociological and political analysis. COVID-19 has involved a continuous struggle, sometimes disguised, other times overt, between the economy and the health needs of ordinary citizens. Feierstein's sophisticated analysis works at three levels: epistemological, emotional, and ethical-moral. His analysis comes alive in terms of his insights into the failed policies of Argentina – a society with a deep commitment to individualism and an historical distrust of state power. At the psycho-analytical dimension, Feierstein uncovers the many responses we make towards catastrophe: denial, projection, and scapegoating. The result is a volume rich in insights into the psychological, social, and political dimensions of the catastrophe that engulfs us."

Bryan S. Turner, *Professor of Sociology and Director of the Institute for Religion, Politics and Society at the Australian Catholic University, Australia, Honorary Professor and Director of the Centre for Citizenship, Social Pluralism and Religious Diversity at Potsdam University, Germany, and Emeritus Professor at the Graduate Center at the City University of New York City (CUNY), USA*

"In this ambitious study, Daniel Feierstein shows how despite its biological origins the COVID-19 pandemic has been an eminently social phenomenon. The book provides original insights into the collective psychology of catastrophes, focusing on the defense mechanisms of denial and projection as prerequisites for citizen responsibility; emotions largely absent in neoliberal consumerist societies promoting selfish individualism and egocentrism. While Feierstein is careful to avoid post-pandemic futurology, his analysis provides valuable insights into the trajectory of the pandemic to date, as well as offering a critique of the social and political limits of responses nested within an individualistic consumer culture."

Greg Martin, *Associate Professor of Criminology, Law and Society, University of Sydney, Australia*

"In *Social and Political Representations of the COVID-19 Crisis*, Dr. Feierstein does a masterful job of examining state responses to the challenges posed by COVID-19 pandemic and the effects these state actions have on various populations in society. Feierstein connects these broad social responses to COVID-19 with individual psychological defense mechanisms people use to cope with a new reality in light of the pandemic. Finally, Dr. Feierstein illustrates how the pandemic can be an opportunity for social change, either positive or negative. This thought-provoking book is a must-read for public health policy-makers and health care professionals."

Dinur Blum, *Lecturer in Sociology, California State University, Los Angeles, USA*